COLOR YOUR OWN!

JAMES PATTERSON

MAX RIDE

PENCILERS

ALEX SANCHEZ & RB SILVA

INKERS

ALEX SANCHEZ, MARK PENNINGTON, WALDEN WONG, RB SILVA, LE BEAU UNDERWOOD, SCOTT HANNA & LARRY WELCH

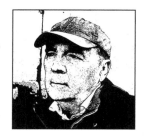

ORIGINAL SERIES EDITORS

CHARLES BEACHAM, SANA AMANAT & EMILY SHAW

ADAPTED FROM THE NOVELS

MAXIMUM RIDE* AND *MAXIMUM RIDE: SCHOOL'S OUT FOREVER

BY JAMES PATTERSON

COLLECTION EDITOR: **JENNIFER GRÜNWALD**
ASSOCIATE EDITOR: **SARAH BRUNSTAD**
ASSOCIATE MANAGING EDITOR: **ALEX STARBUCK**
EDITOR, SPECIAL PROJECTS: **MARK D. BEAZLEY**
VP, PRODUCTION & SPECIAL PROJECTS: **JEFF YOUNGQUIST**
SVP PRINT, SALES & MARKETING: **DAVID GABRIEL**
BOOK DESIGNER: **ADAM DEL RE**
EDITOR IN CHIEF: **AXEL ALONSO**
CHIEF CREATIVE OFFICER: **JOE QUESADA**
PUBLISHER: **DAN BUCKLEY**
EXECUTIVE PRODUCER: **ALAN FINE**

COLOR YOUR OWN JAMES PATTERSON. First printing 2016. ISBN# 978-1-302-90088-5. Published by MARVEL WORLDWIDE, INC., a subsidiary of MARVEL ENTERTAINMENT, LLC. OFFICE OF PUBLICATION: 135 West 50th Street, New York, NY 10020.

Printed in the U.S.A. ALAN FINE, President, Marvel Entertainment; DAN BUCKLEY, President, TV, Publishing & Brand Management; JOE QUESADA, Chief Creative Officer; TOM BREVOORT, SVP of Publishing; DAVID BOGART, SVP of Business Affairs & Operations, Publishing & Partnership; C.B. CEBULSKI, VP of Brand Management & Development, Asia; DAVID GABRIEL, SVP of Sales & Marketing, Publishing; JEFF YOUNGQUIST, VP of Production & Special Projects; DAN CARR, Executive Director of Publishing Technology; ALEX MORALES, Director of Publishing Operations; SUSAN CRESPI, Production Manager; STAN LEE, Chairman Emeritus. For information regarding advertising in Marvel Comics or on Marvel.com, please contact Vit DeBellis, Integrated Sales Manager, at vdebellis@marvel.com. For Marvel subscription inquiries, please call 888-511-5480. **Manufactured between 4/29/2016 and 6/6/2016 by SHERIDAN, CHELSEA, MI, USA.**

10 9 8 7 6 5 4 3 2 1

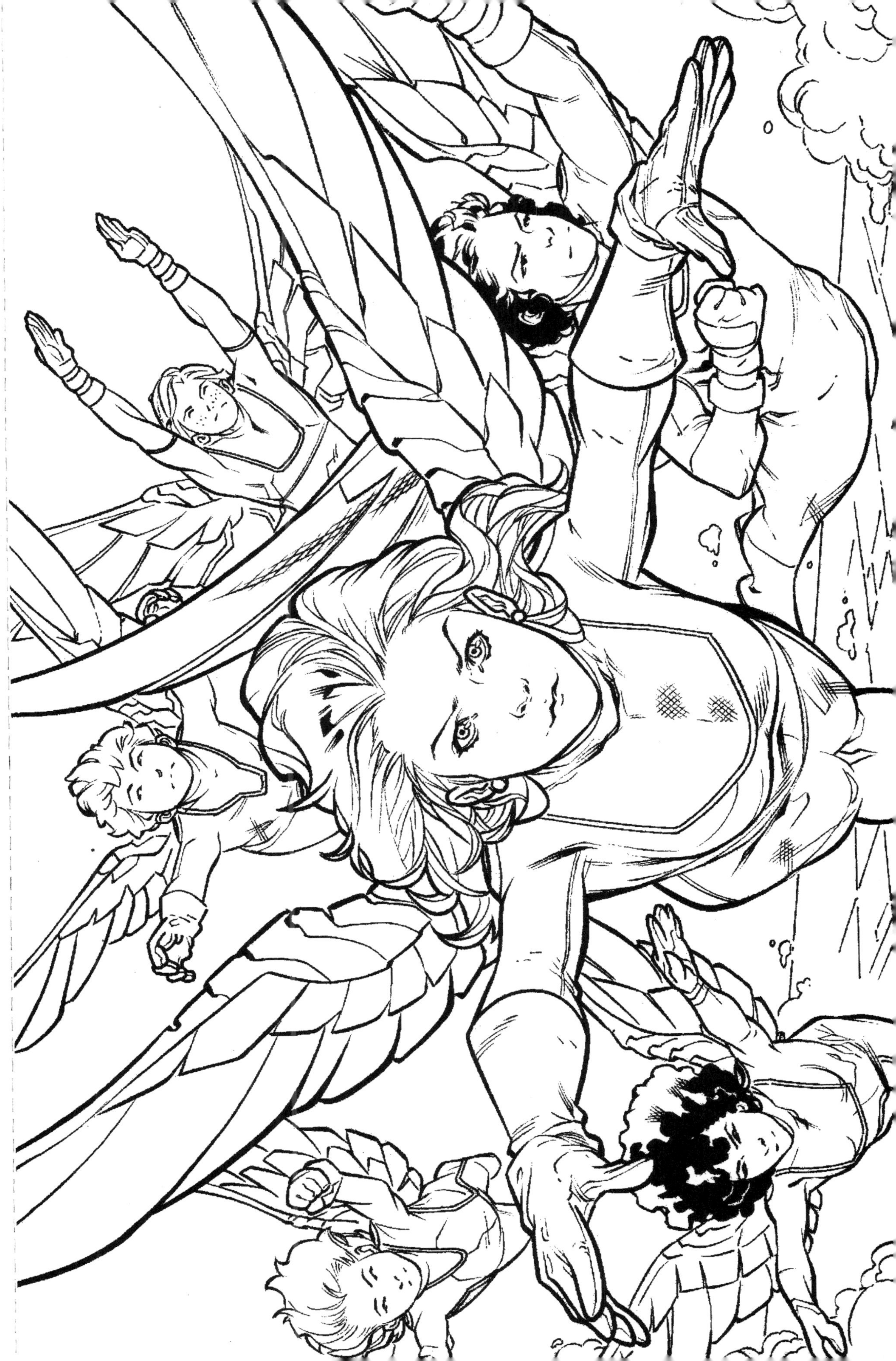

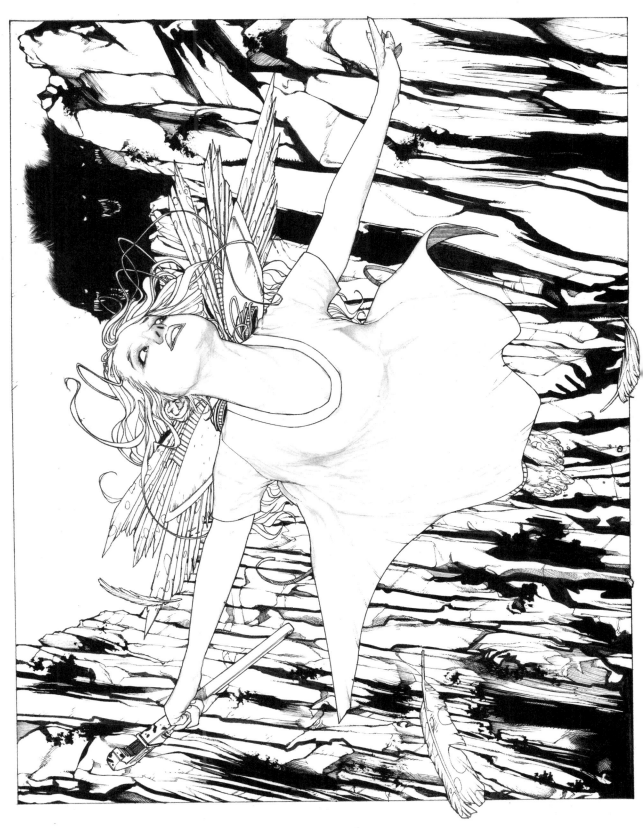

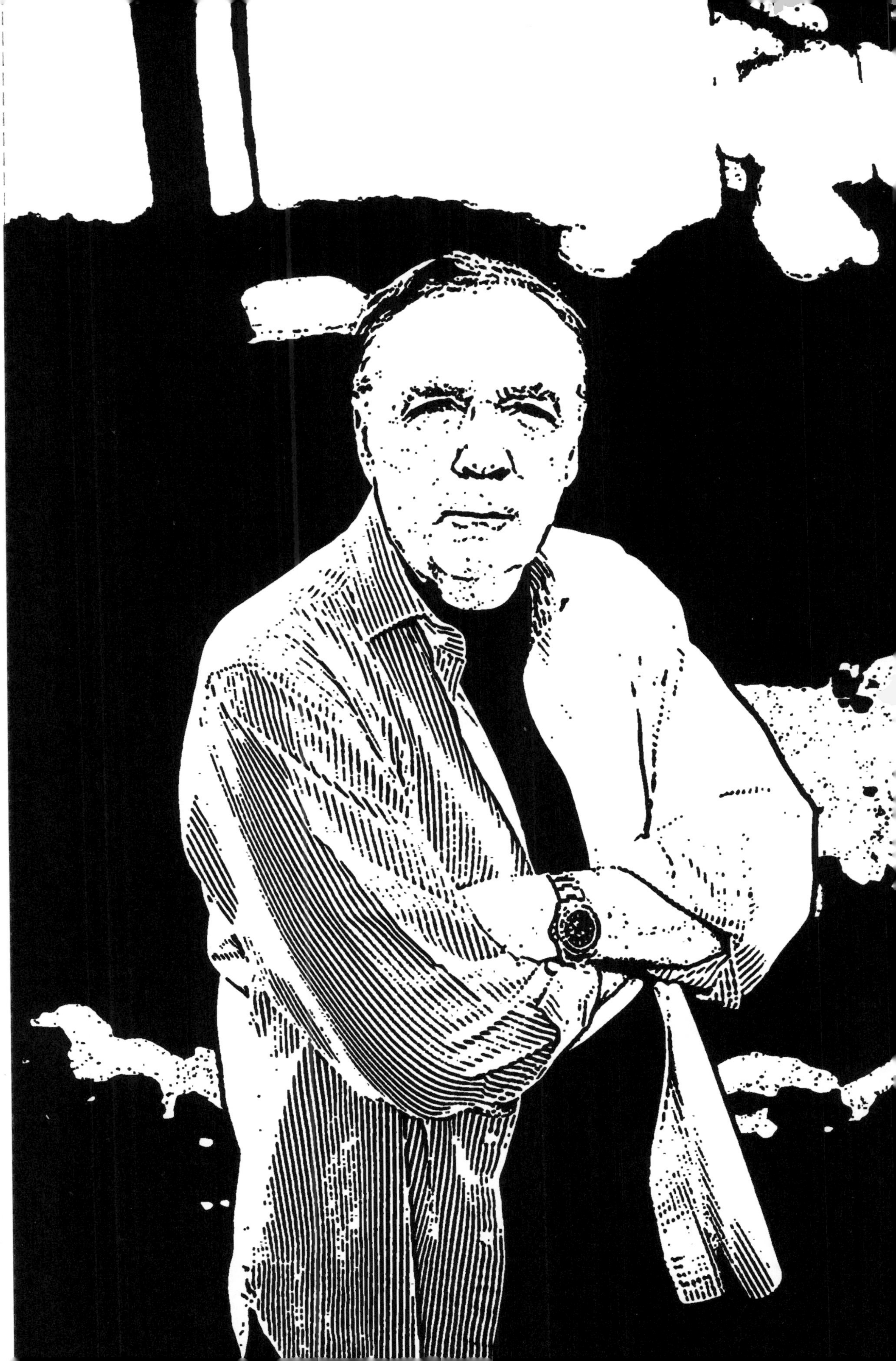

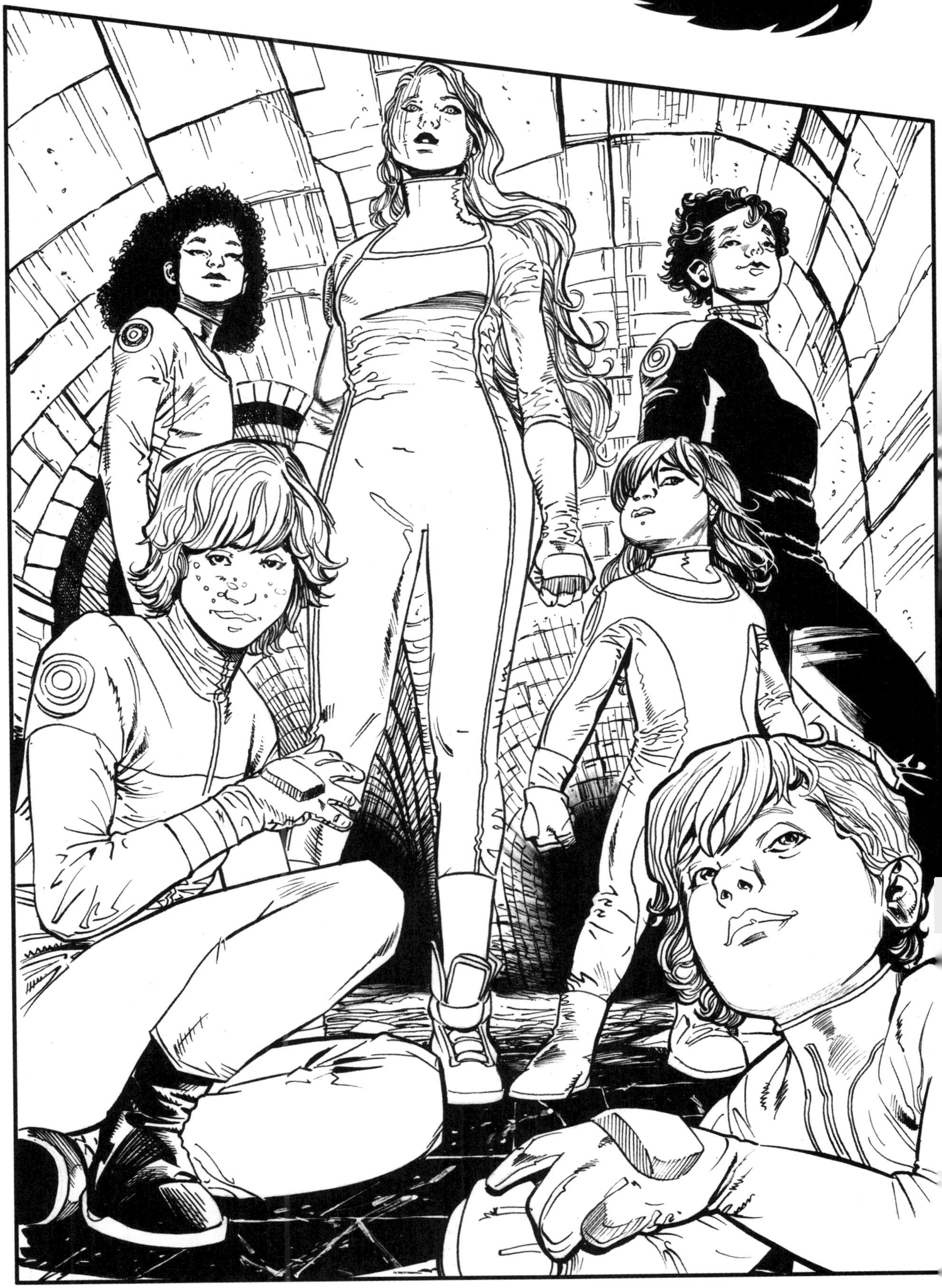

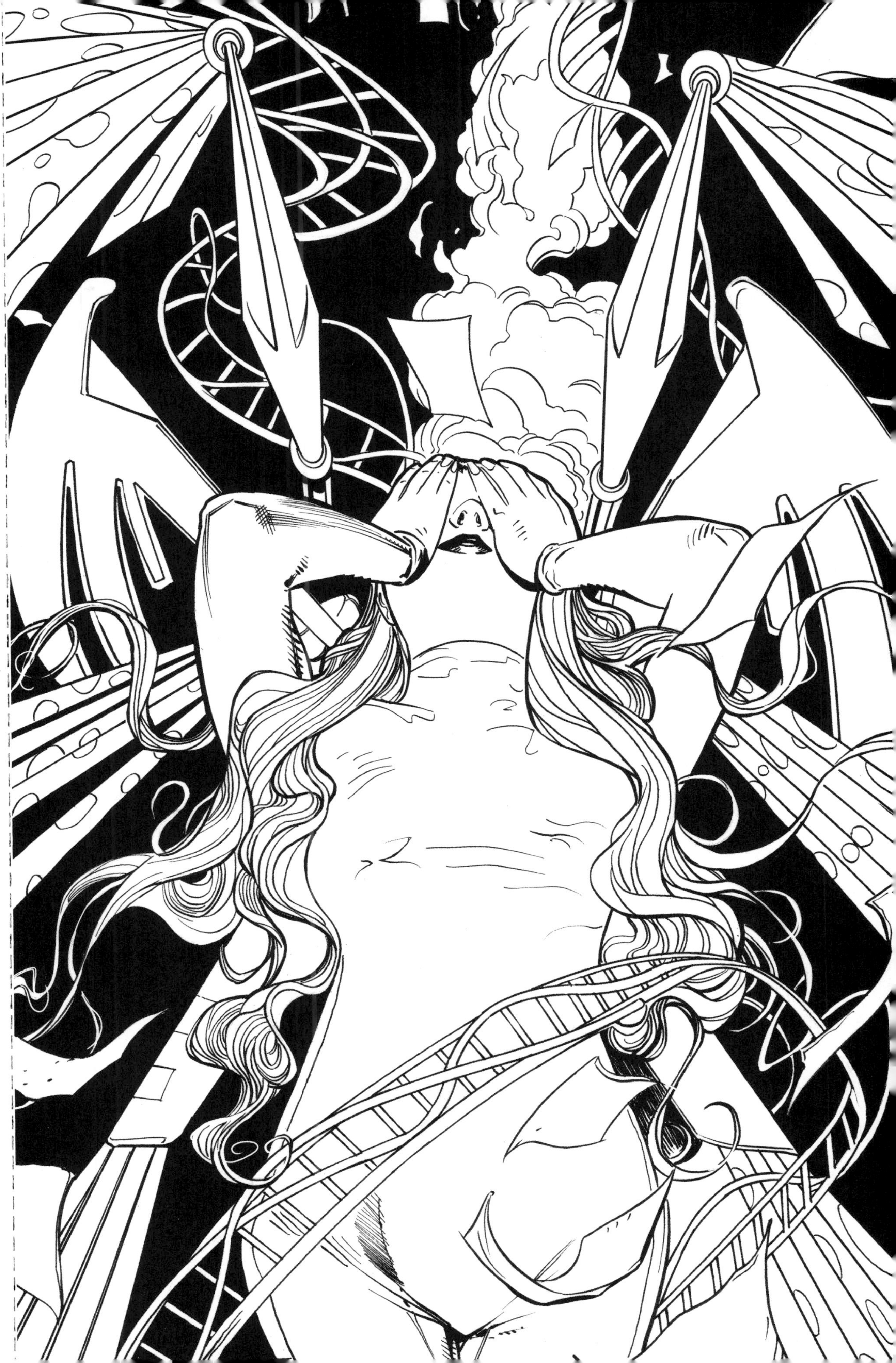

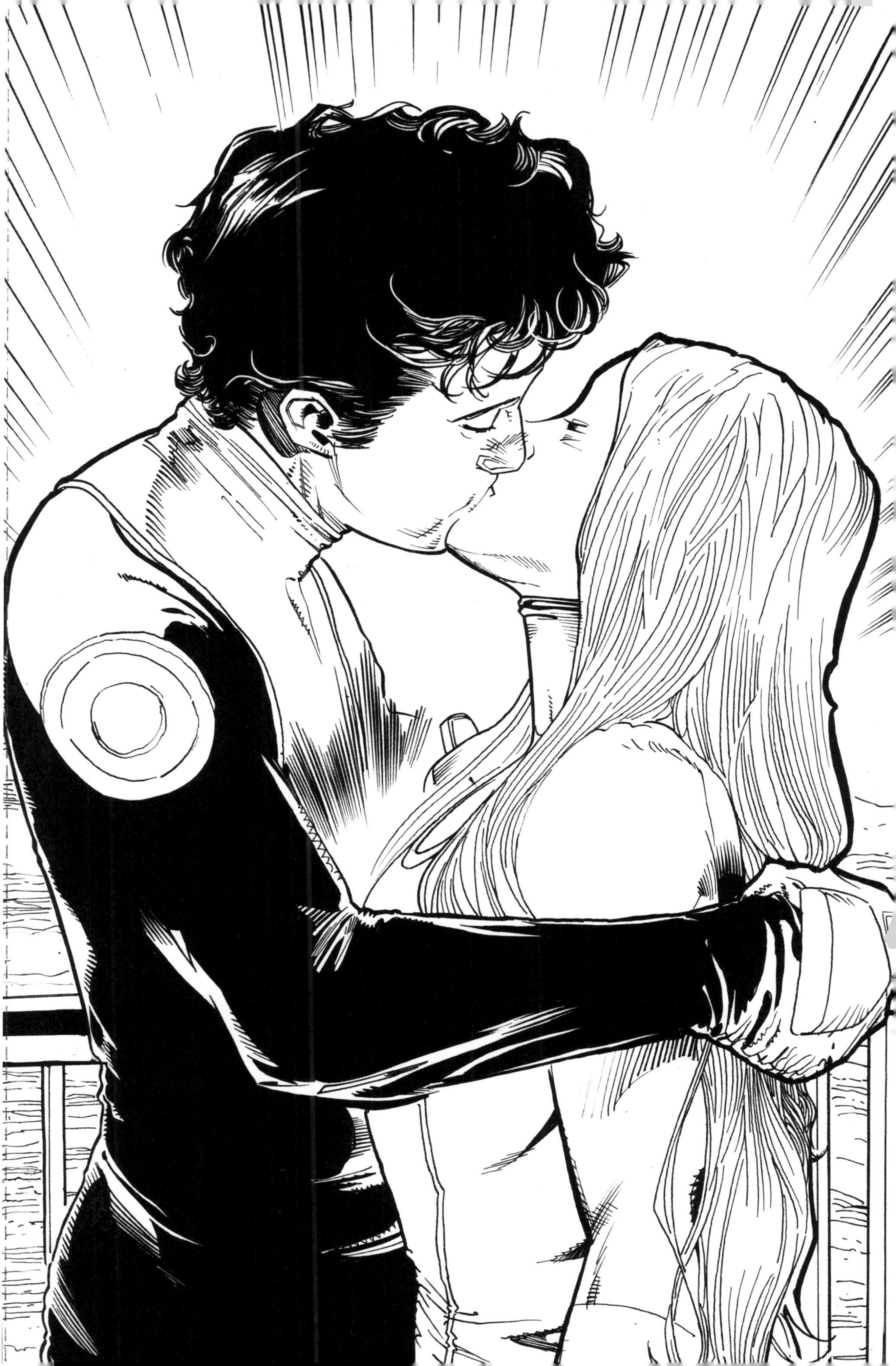

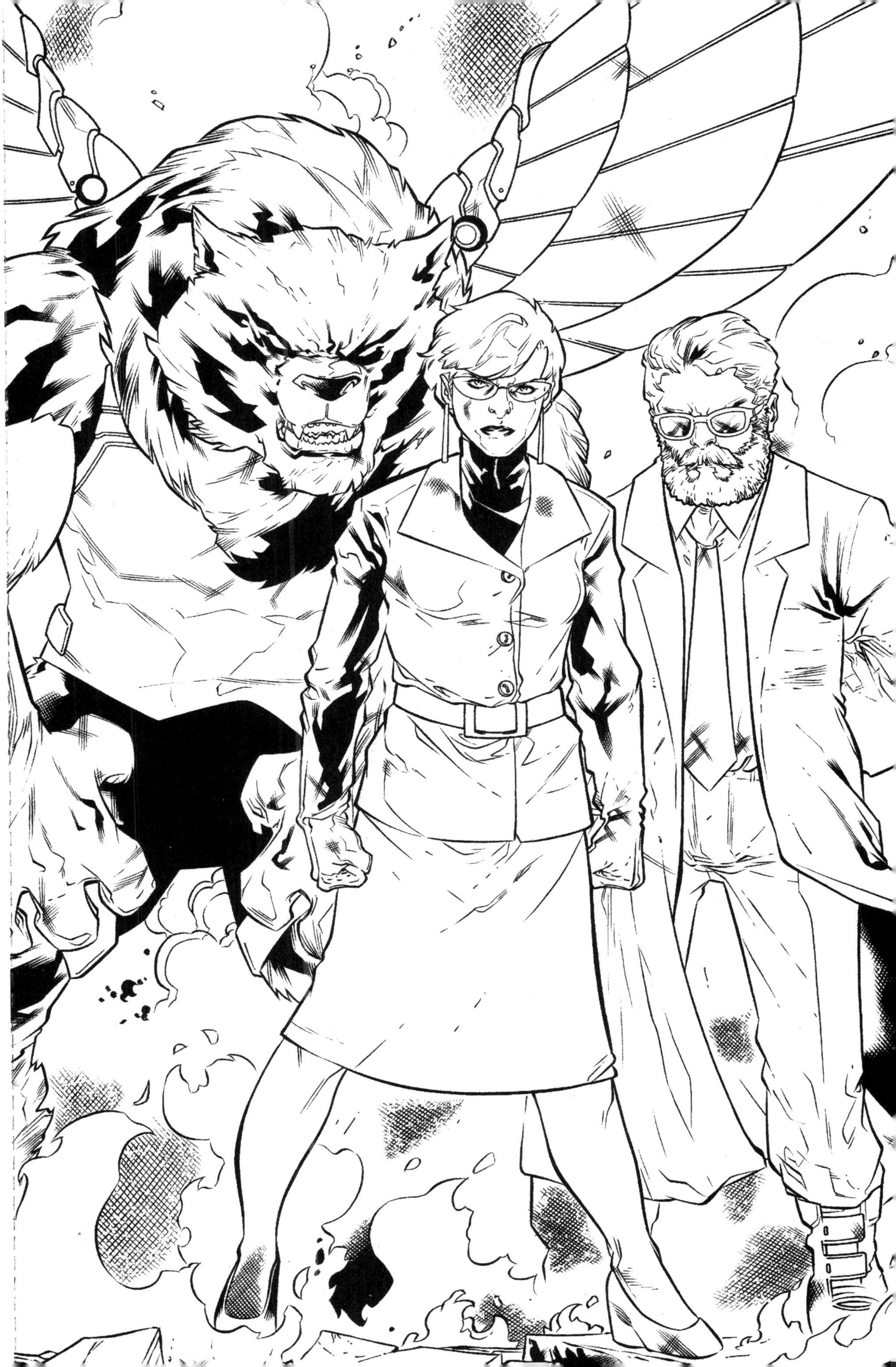

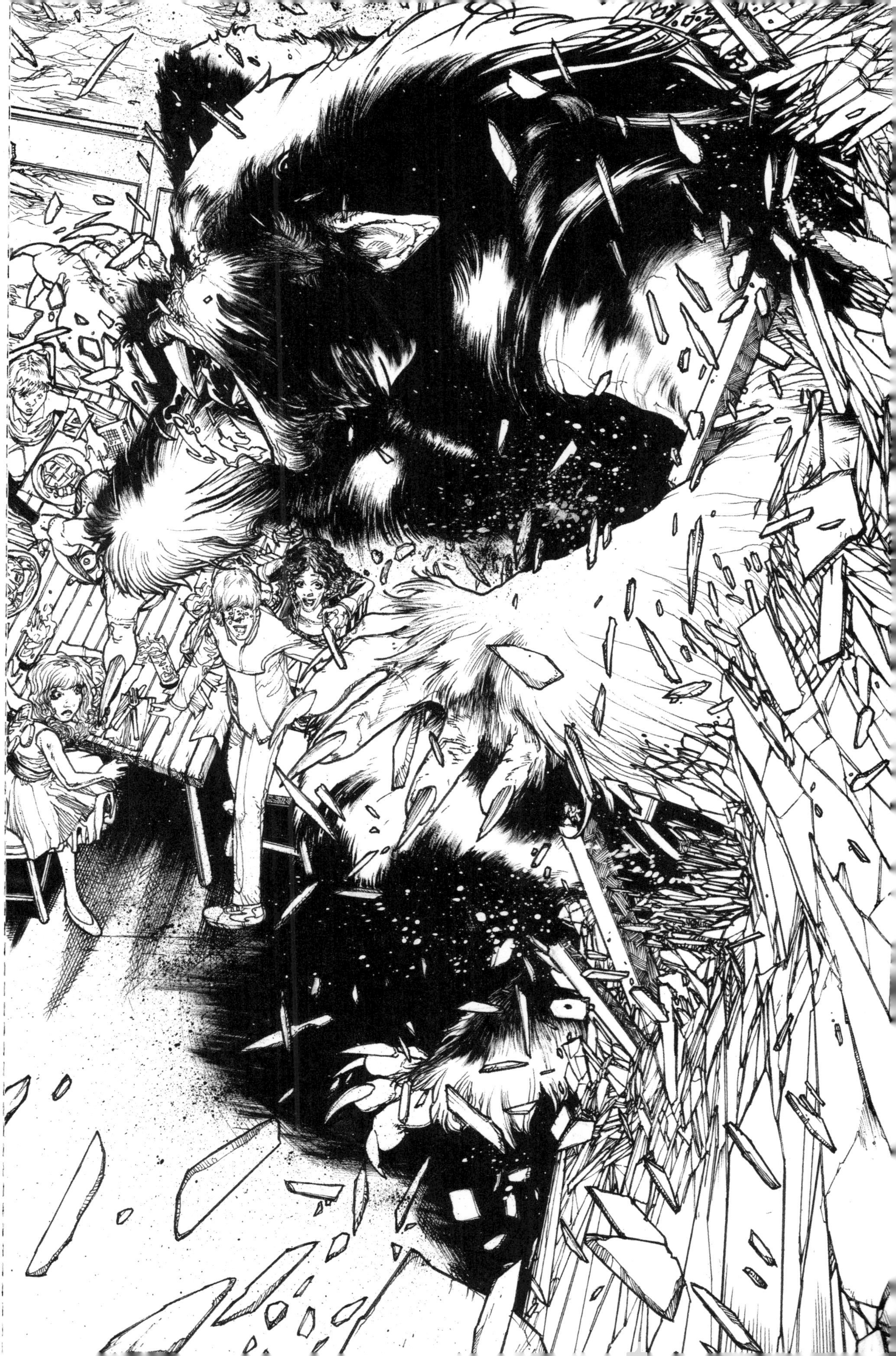

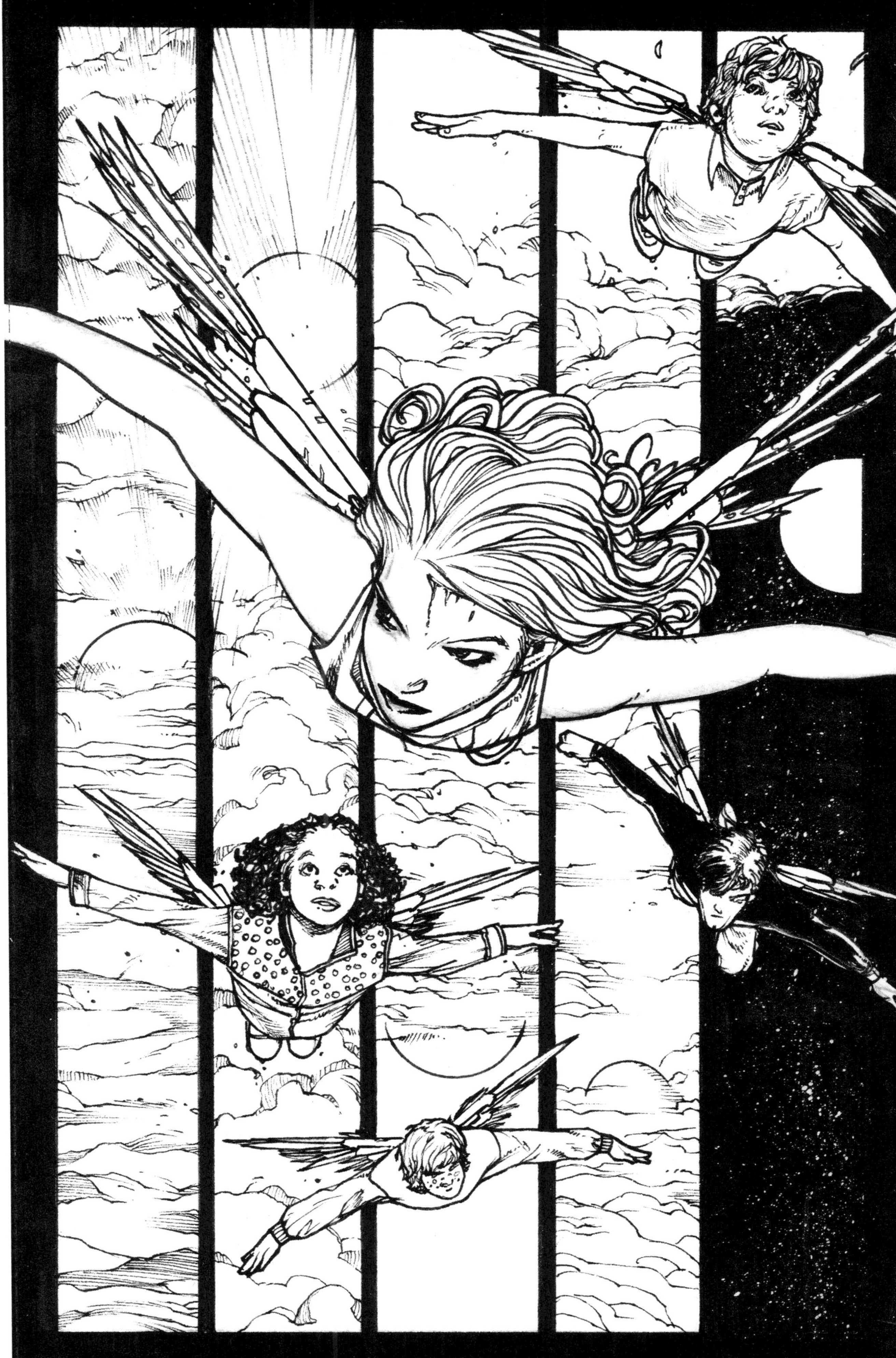

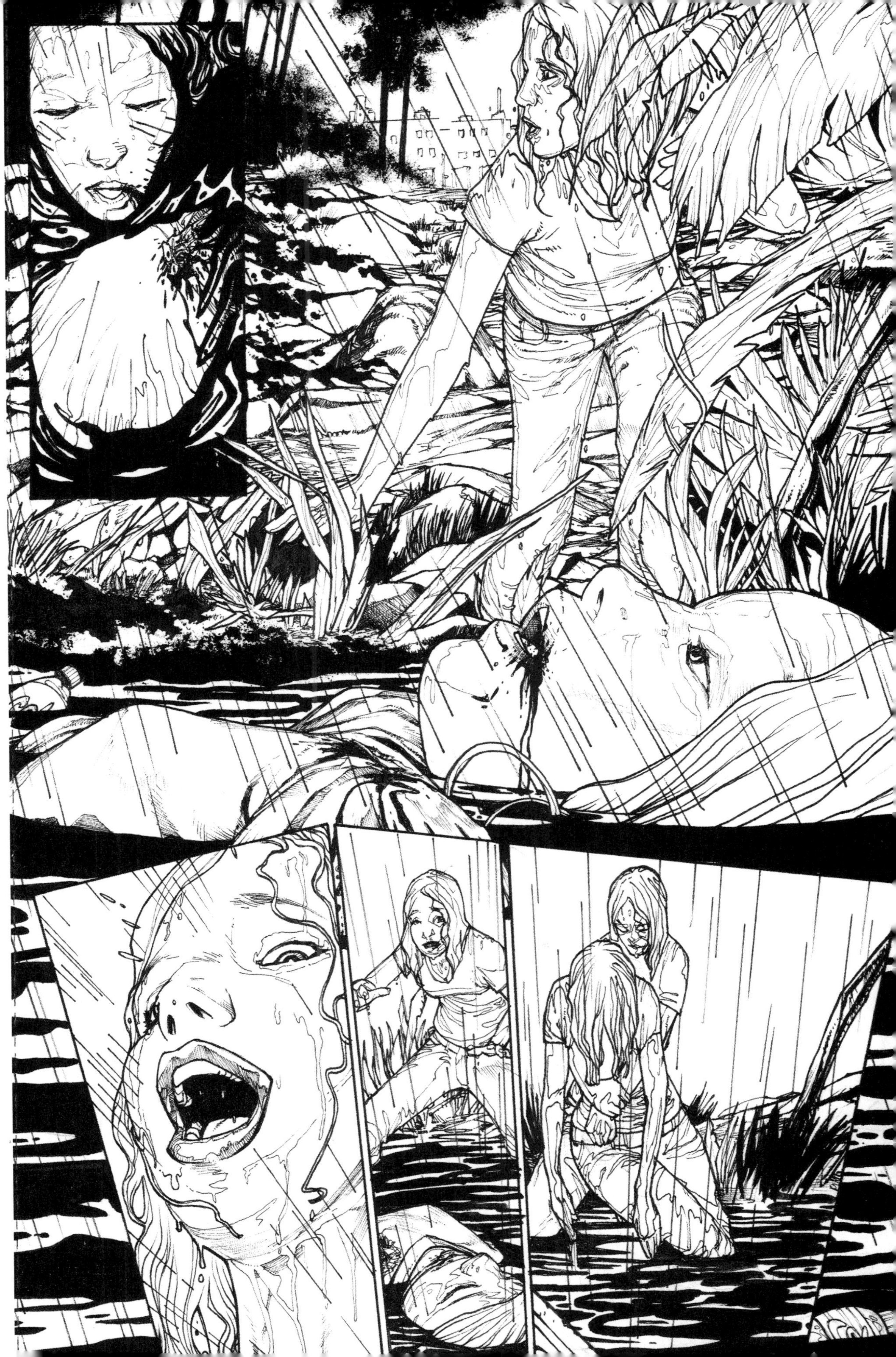

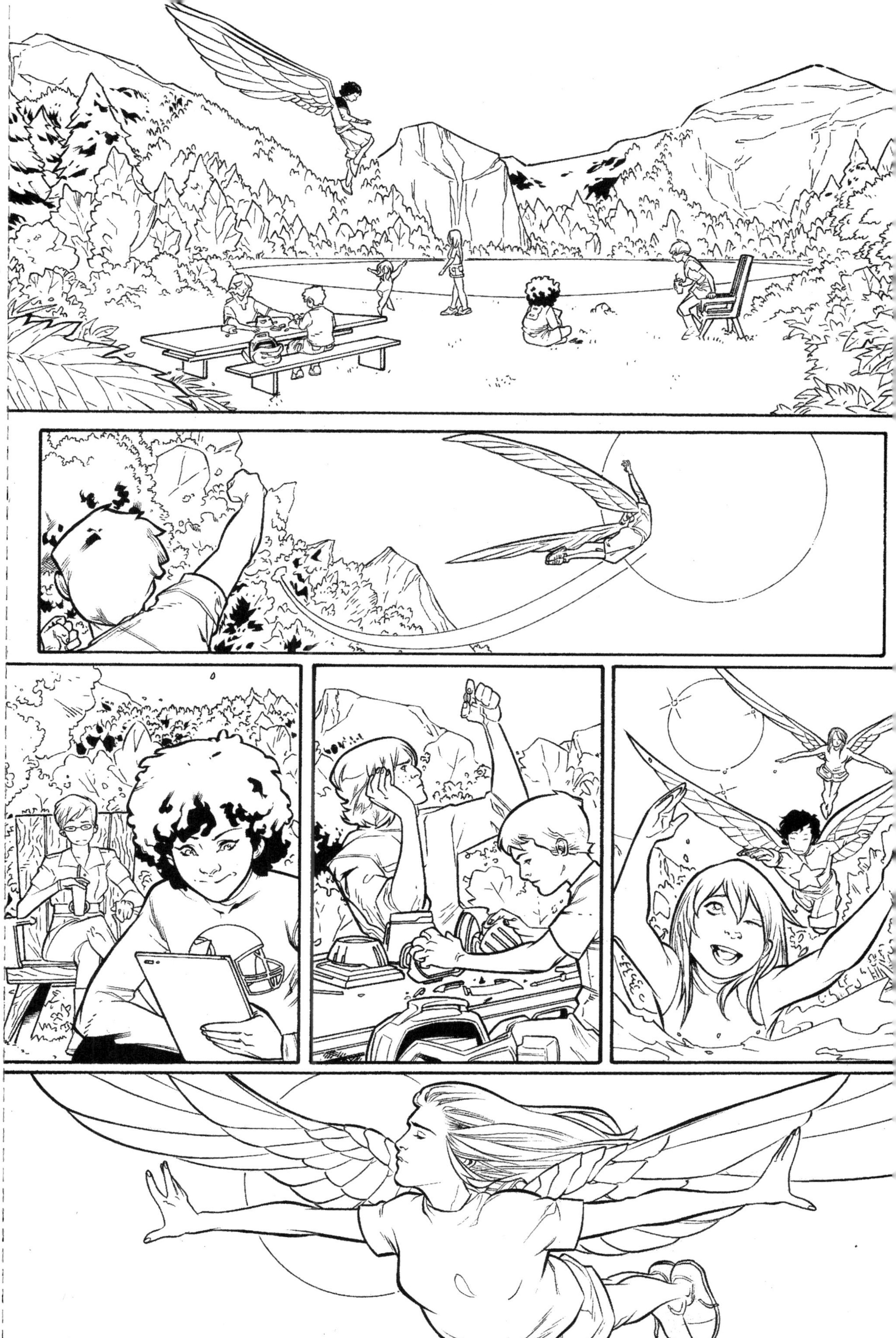

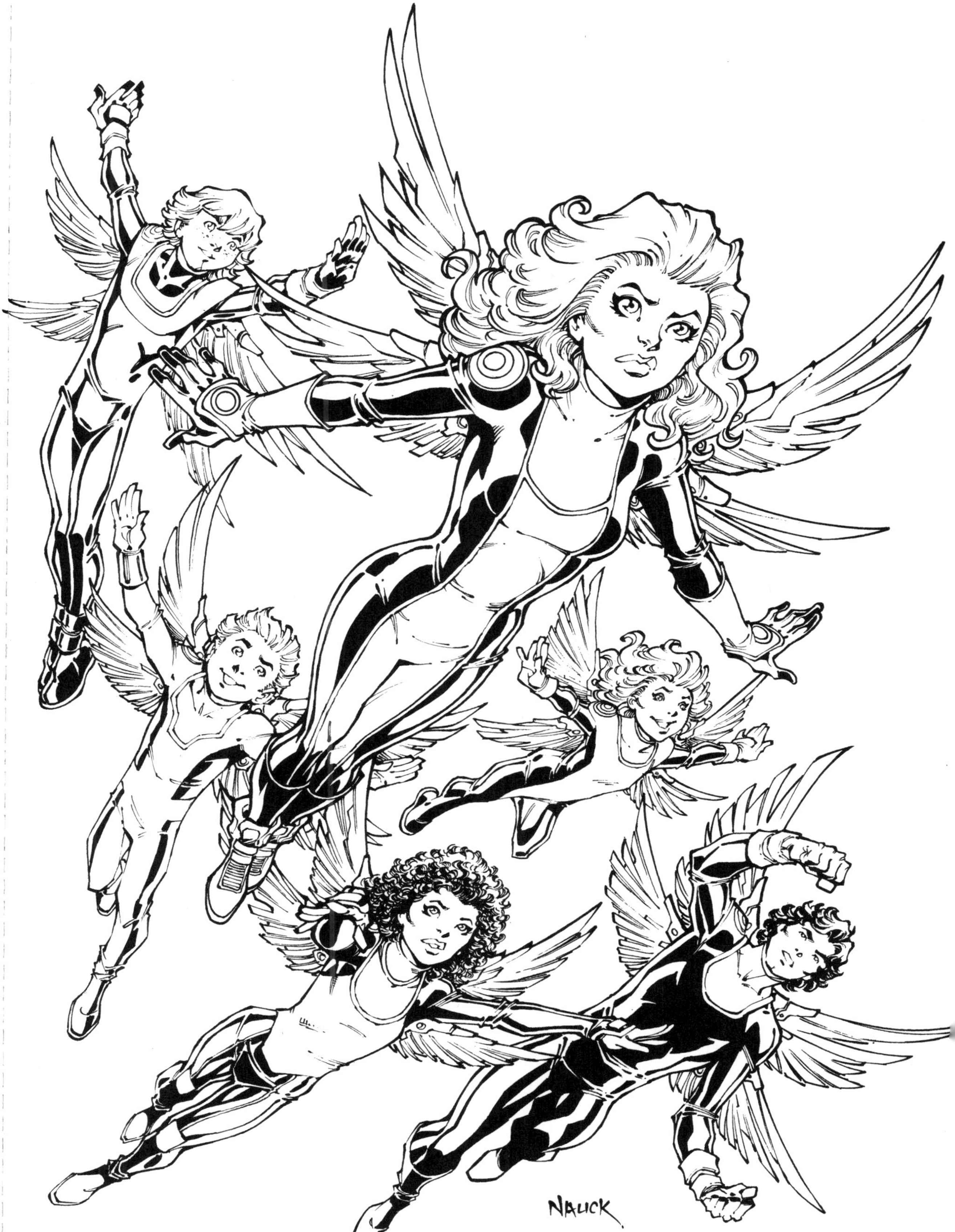
NAUCK

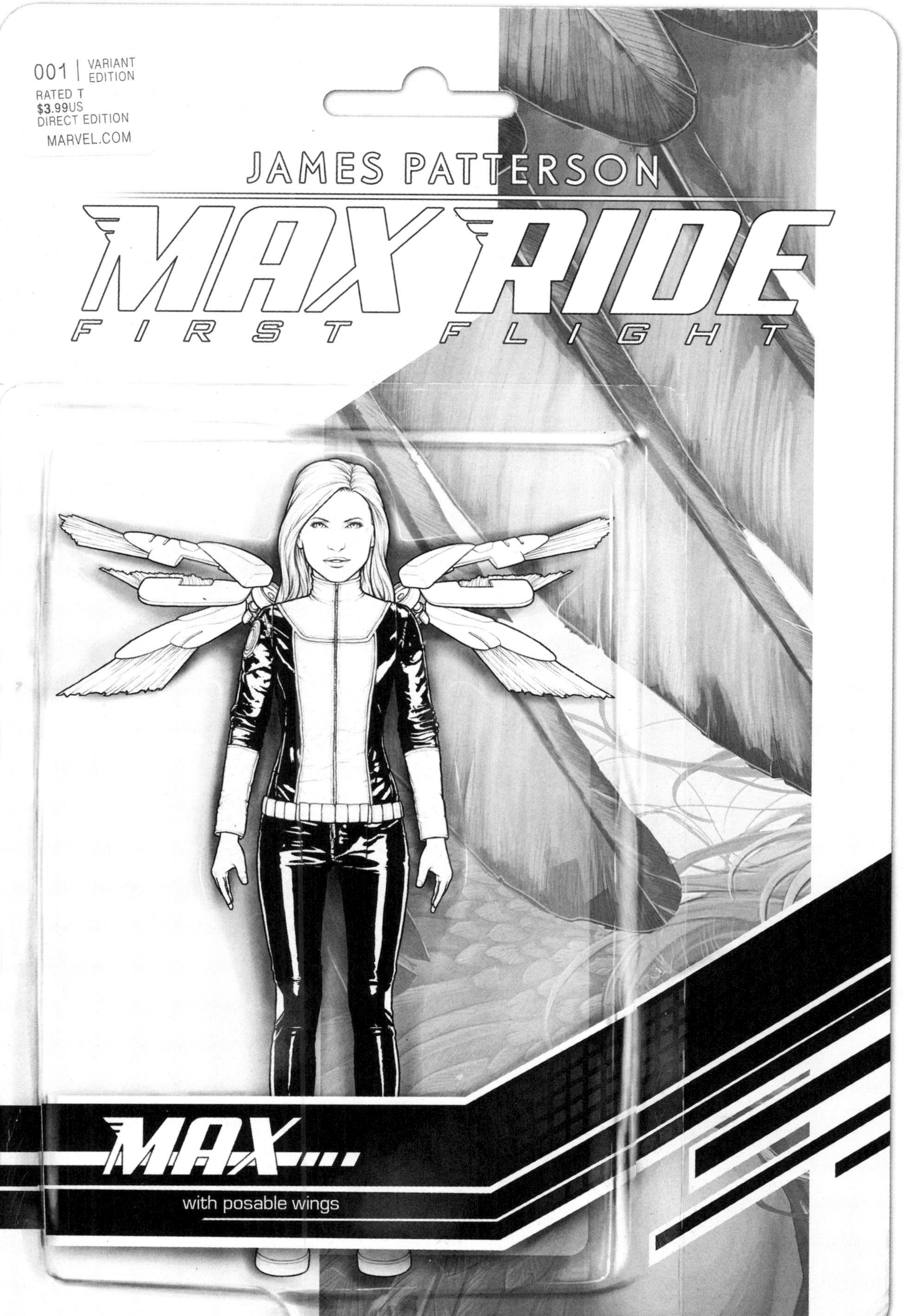
001 | VARIANT EDITION
RATED T
$3.99US
DIRECT EDITION
MARVEL.COM
JAMES PATTERSON
MAX RIDE
FIRST FLIGHT
MAX...
with posable wings

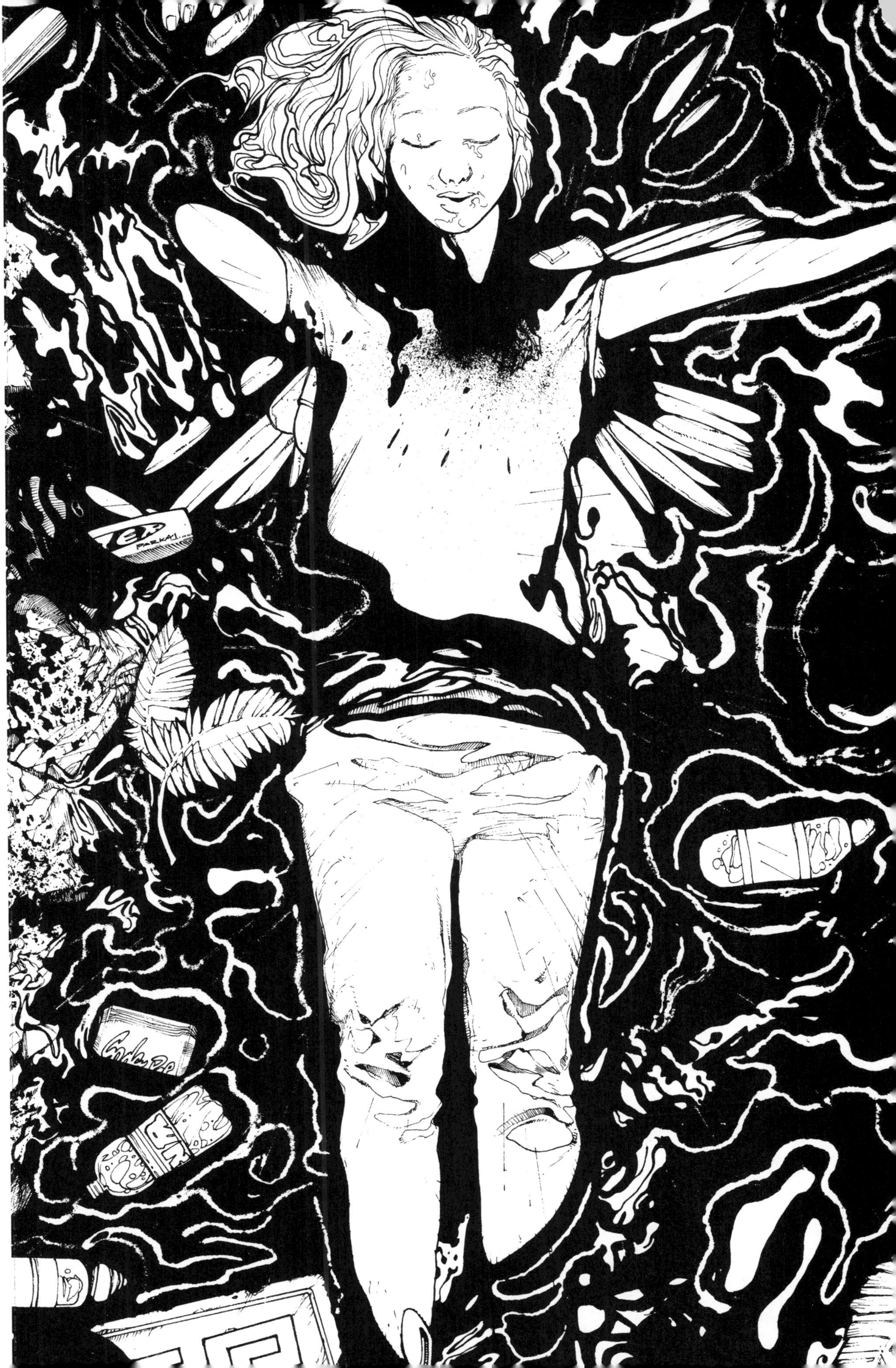

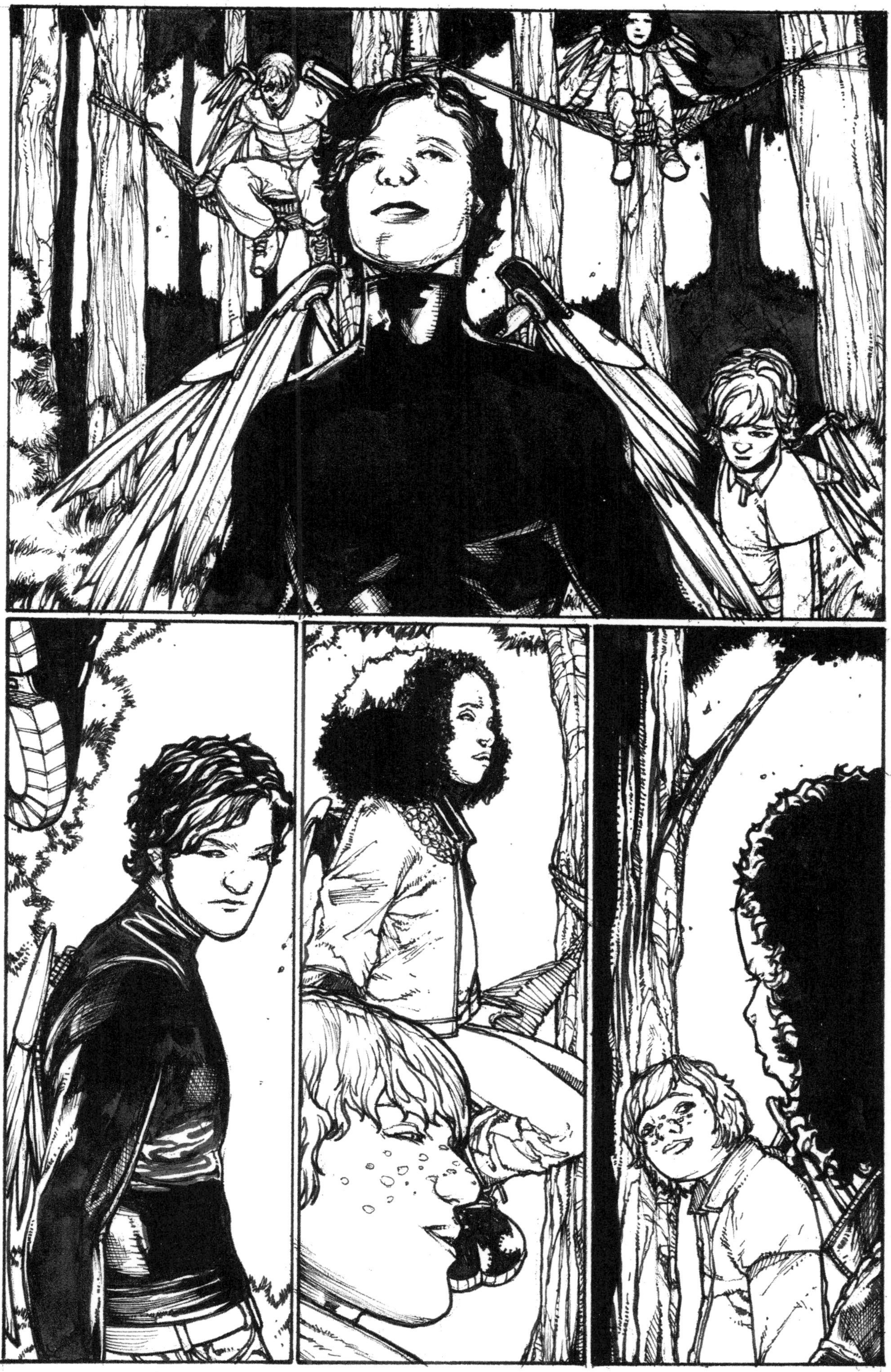

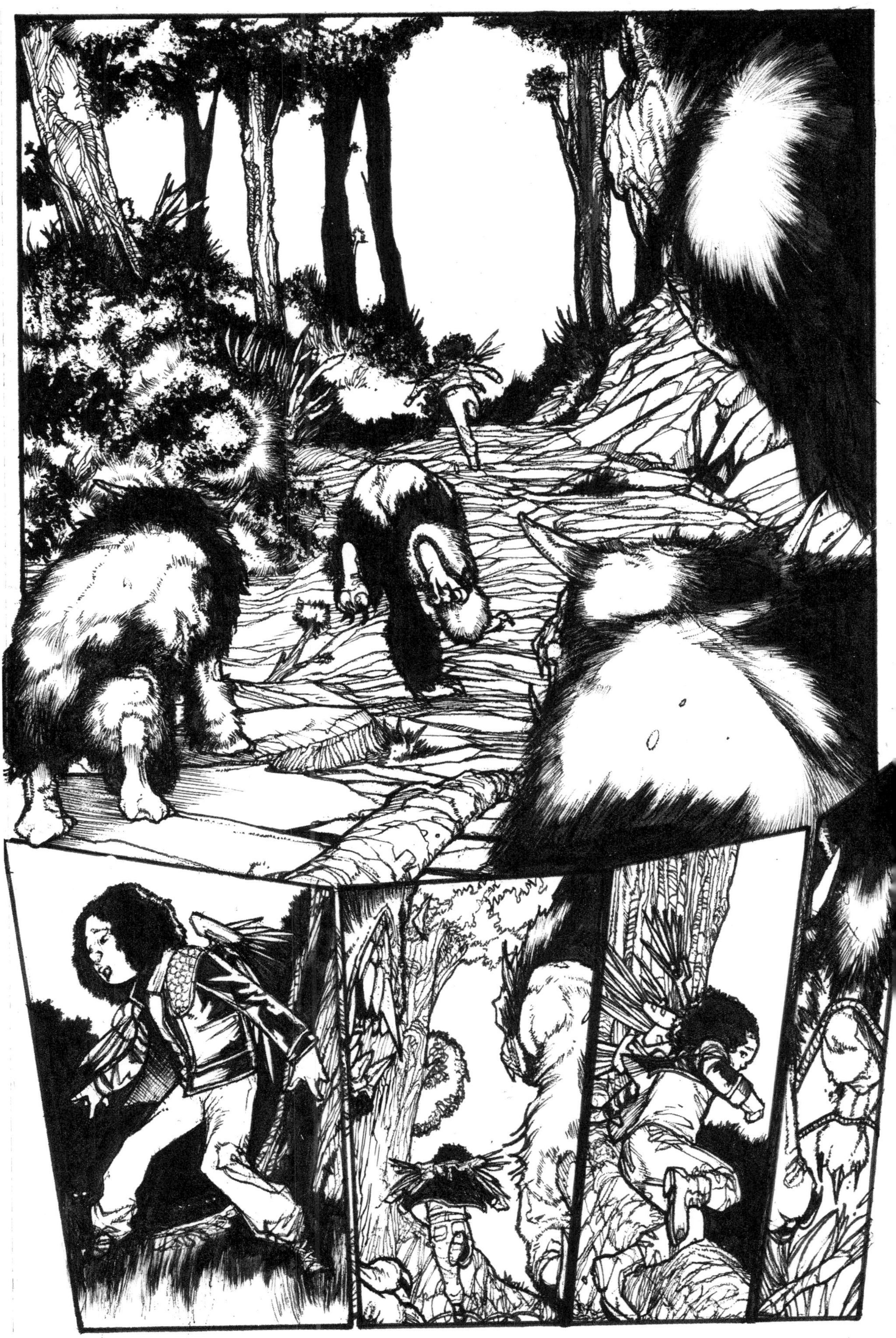

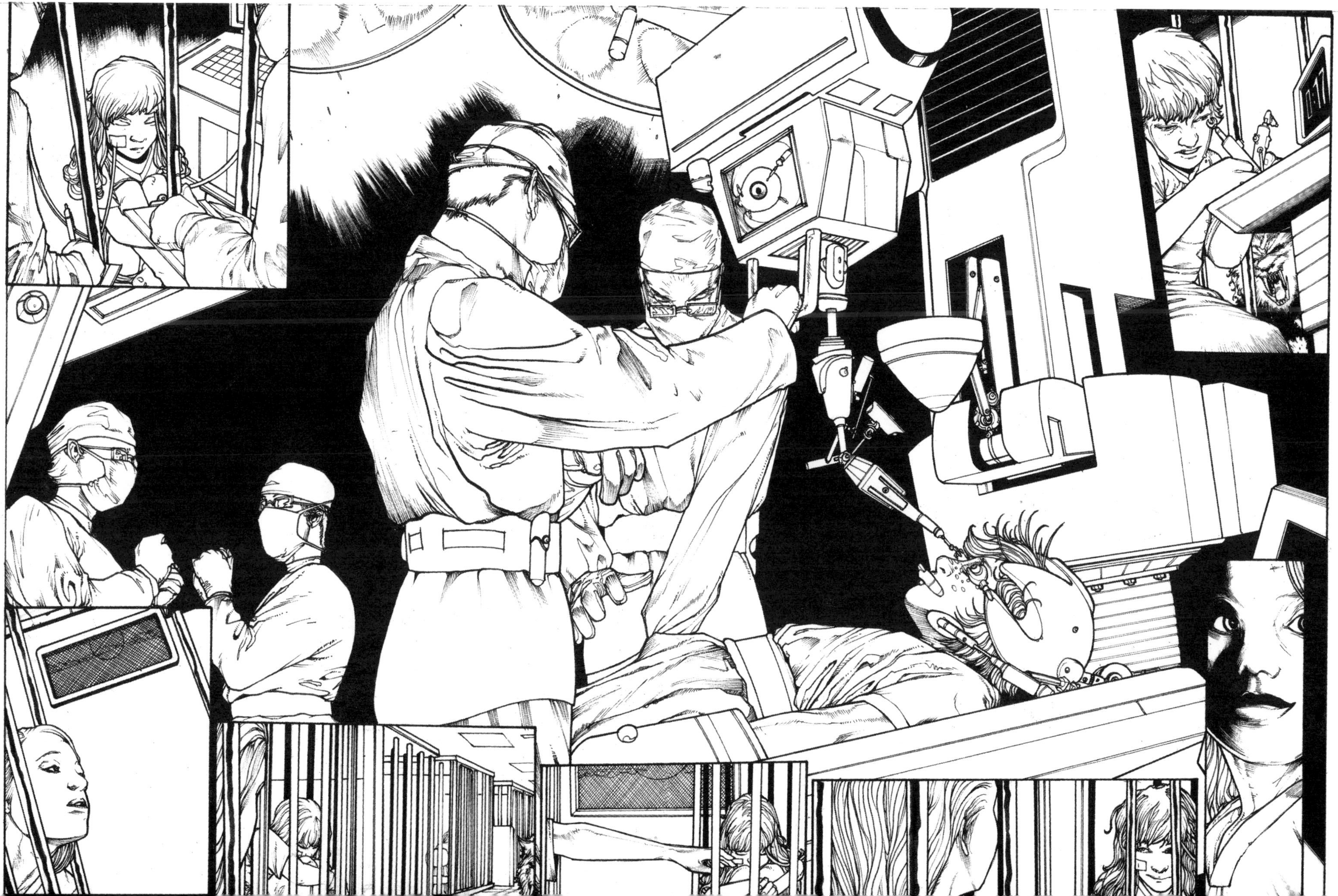

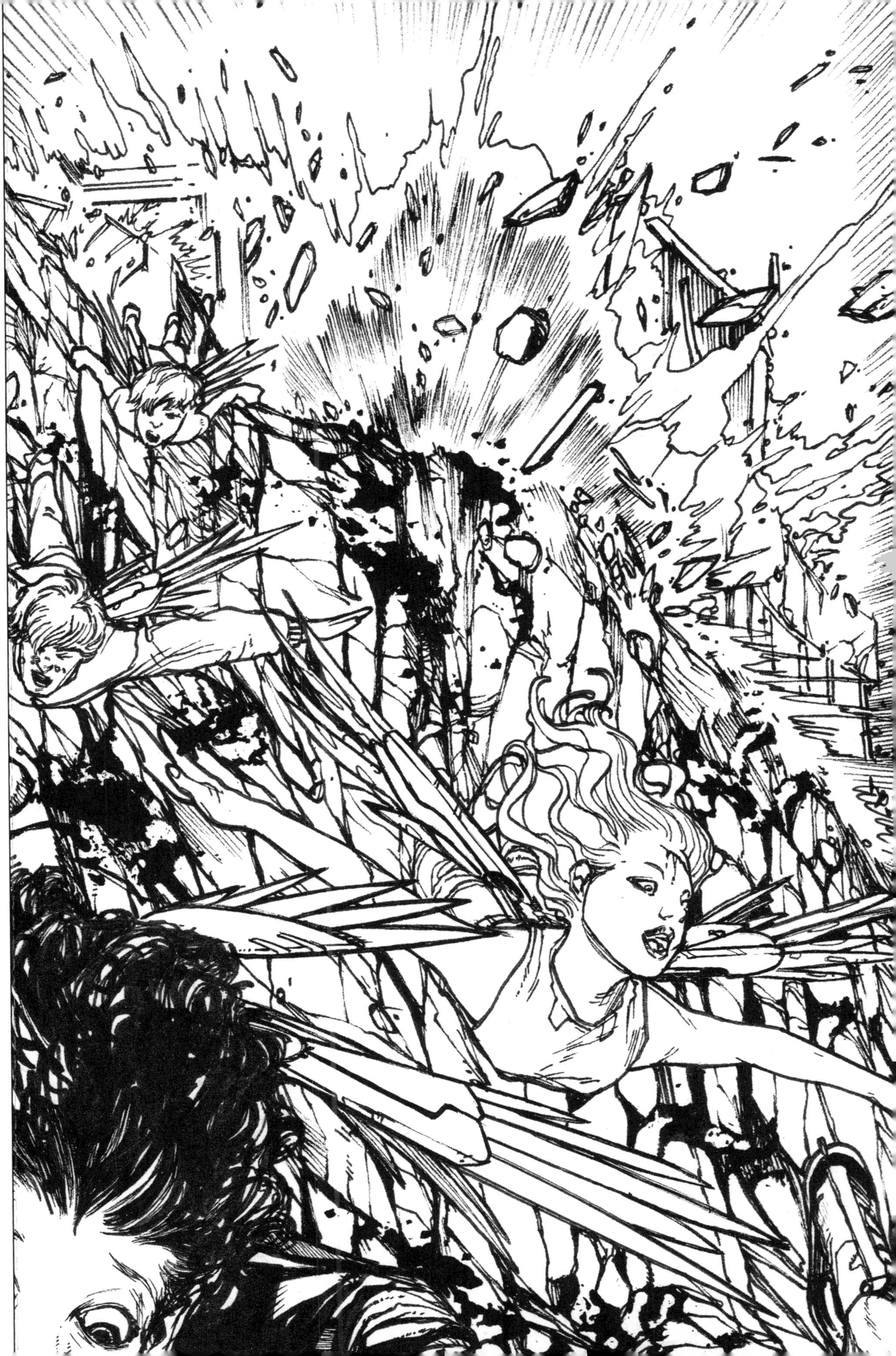

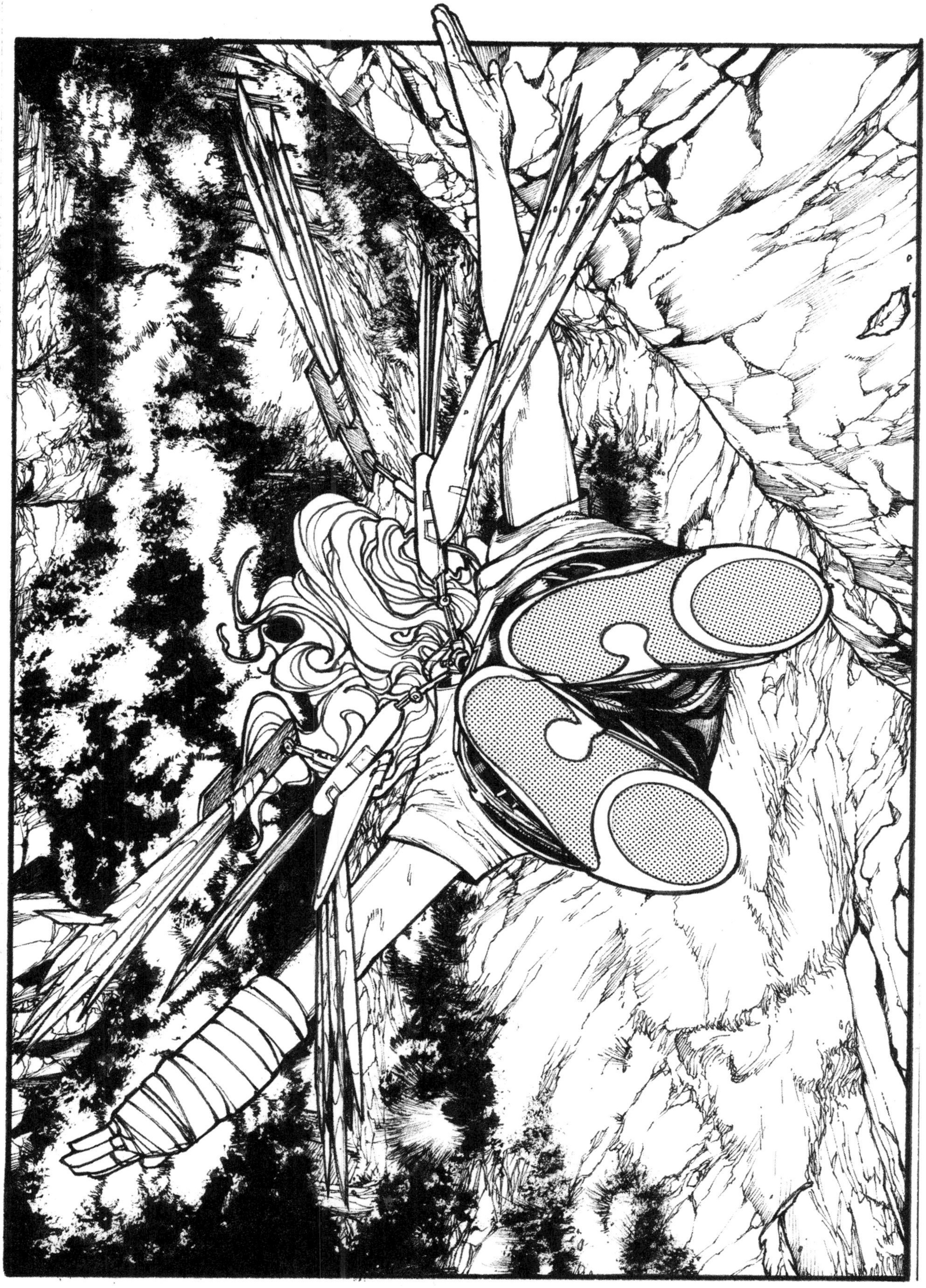

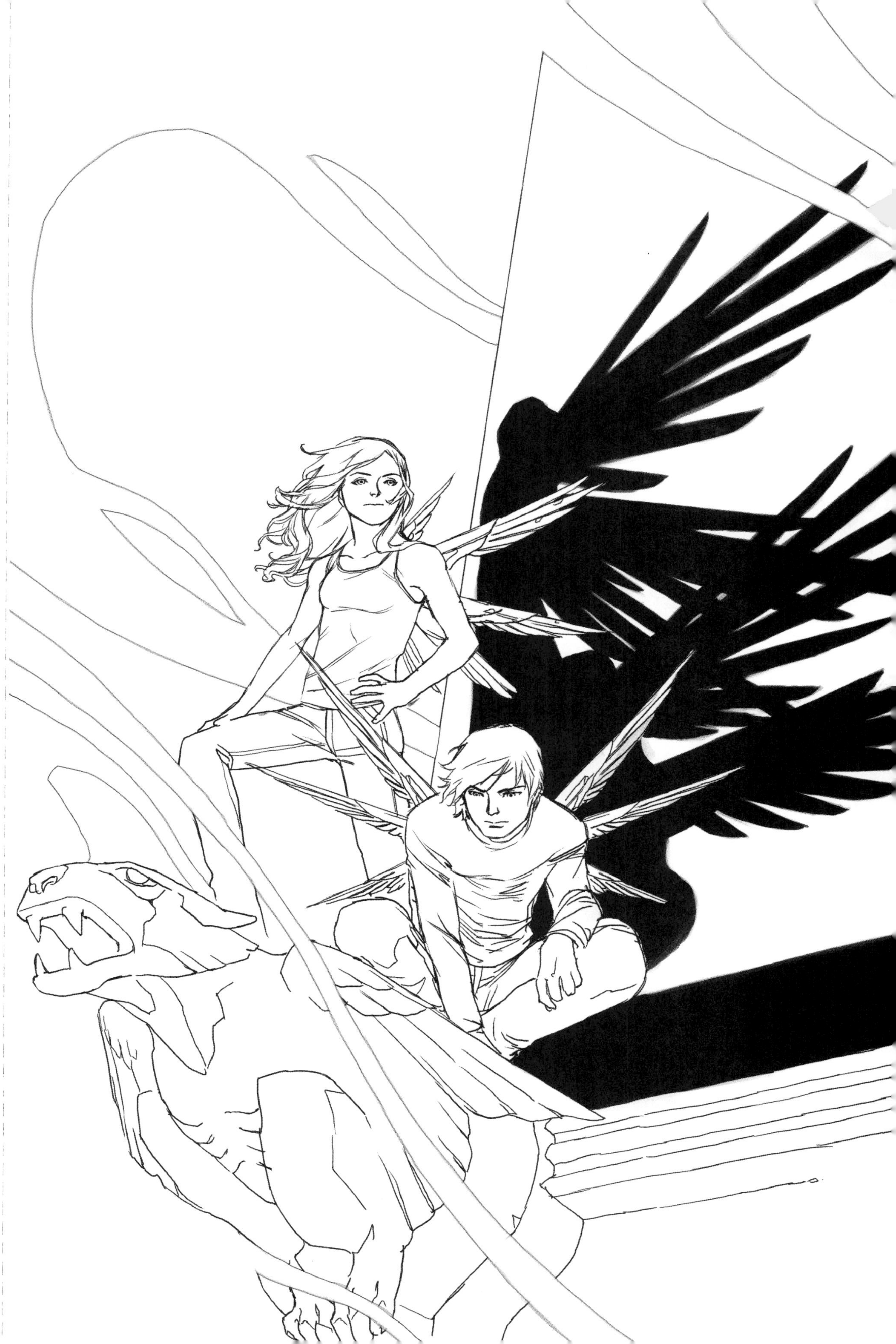

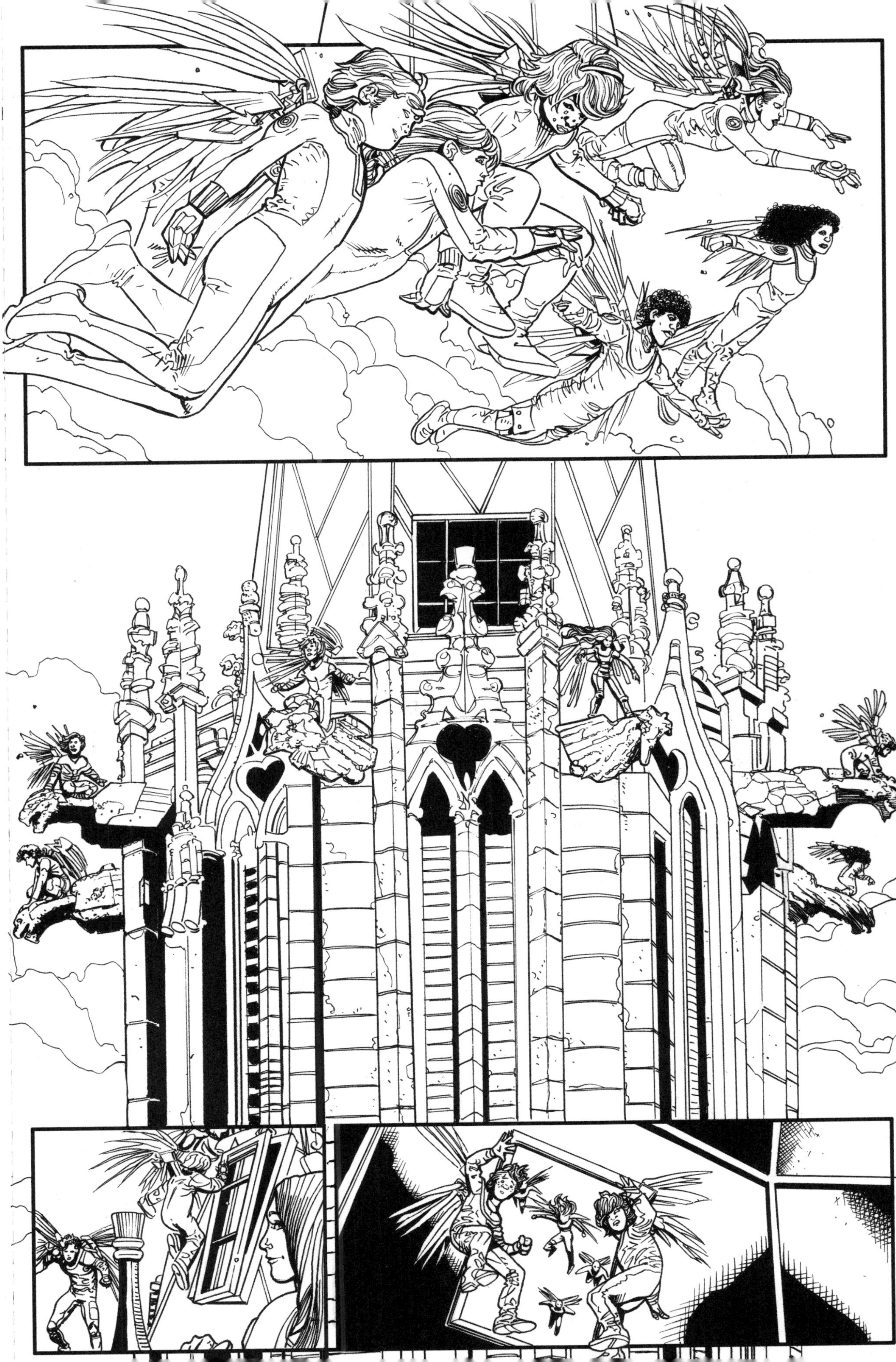

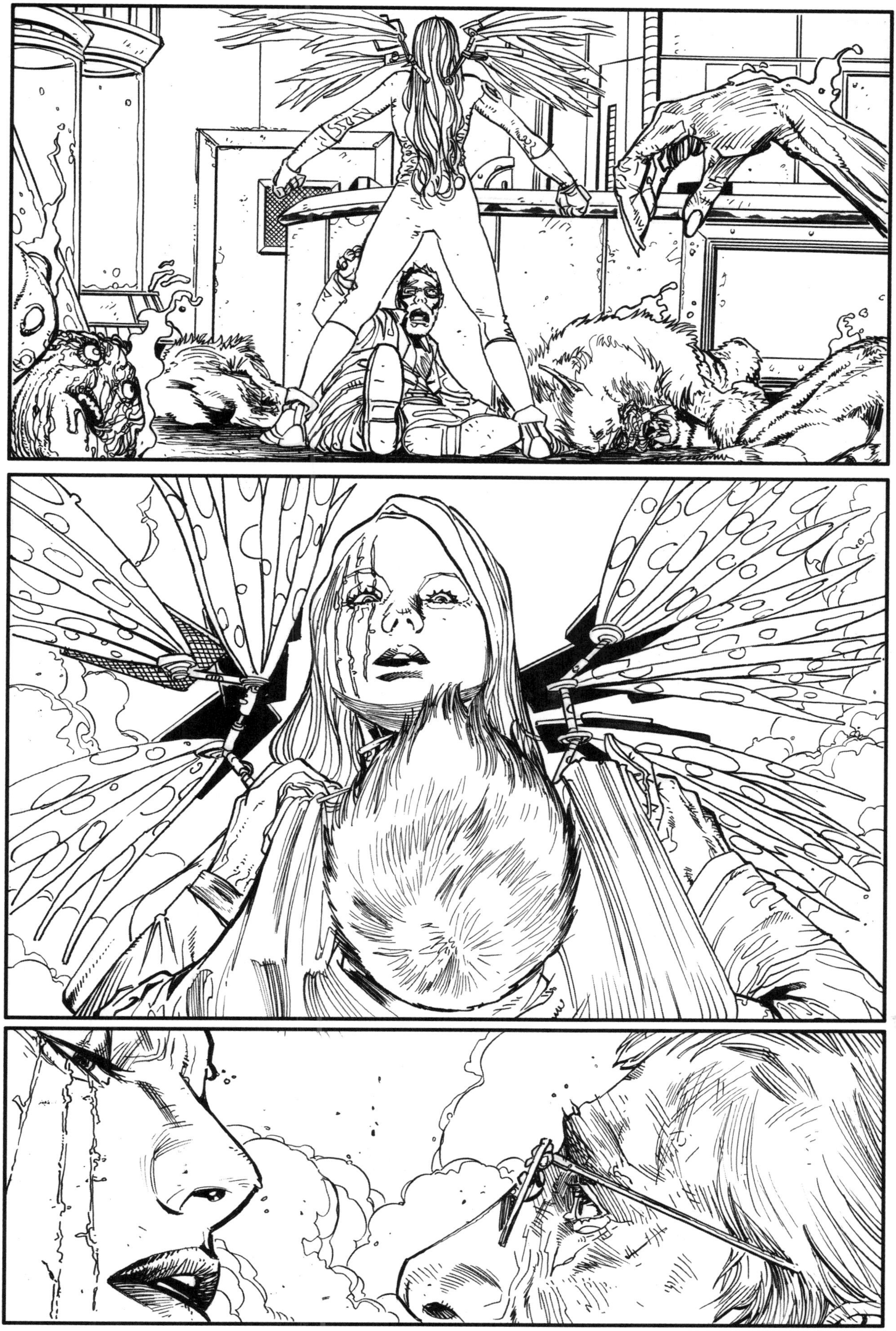

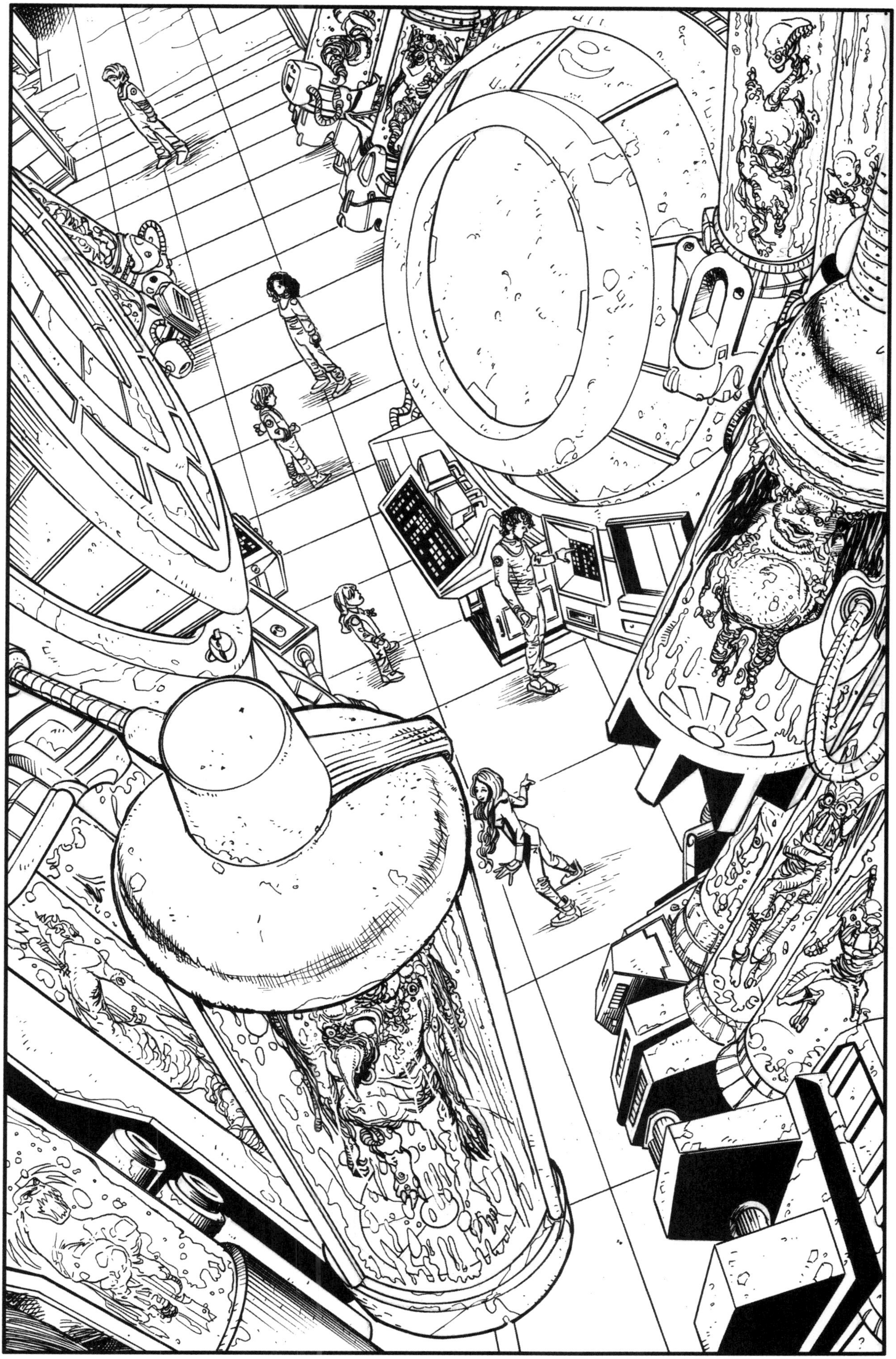

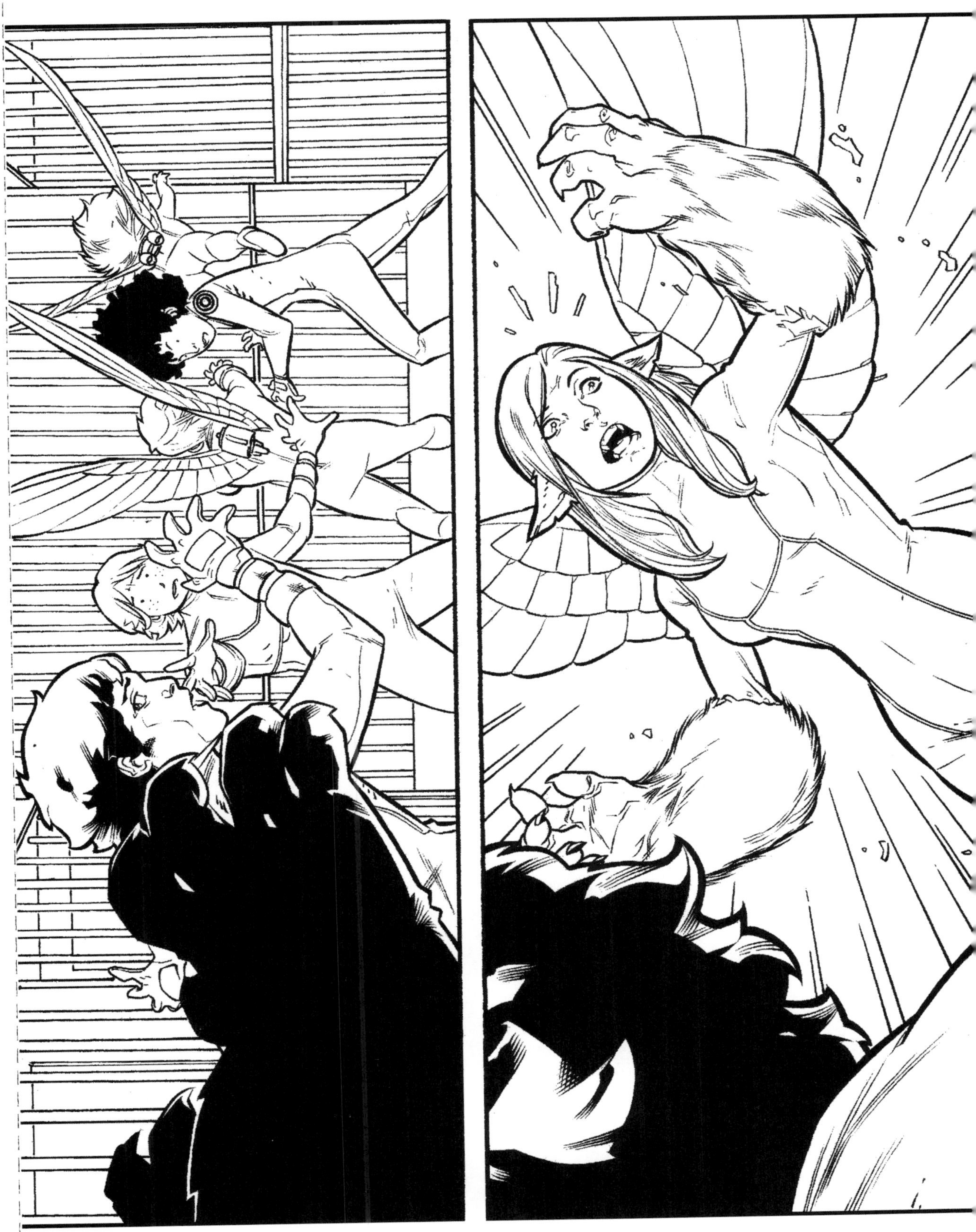

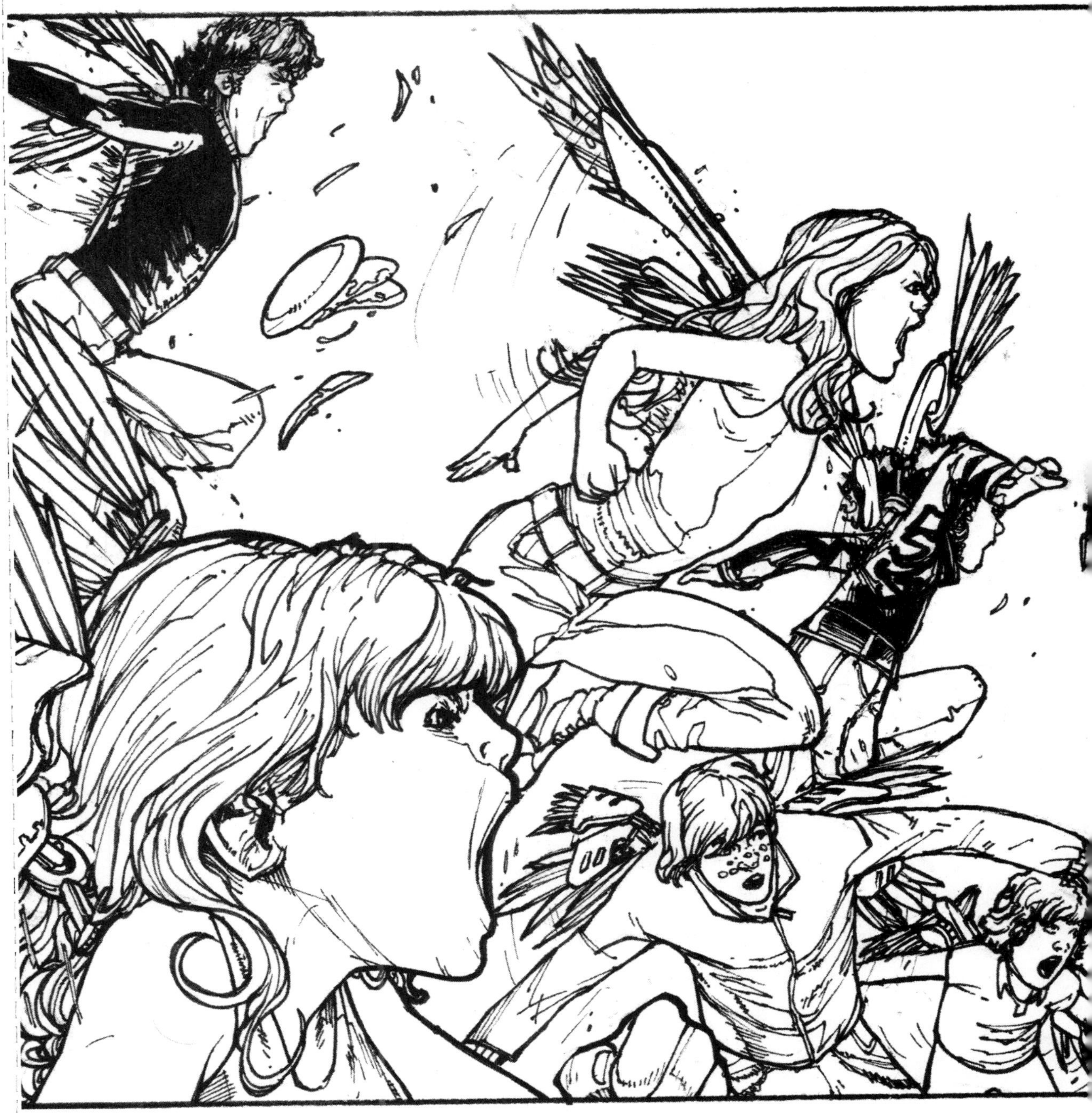

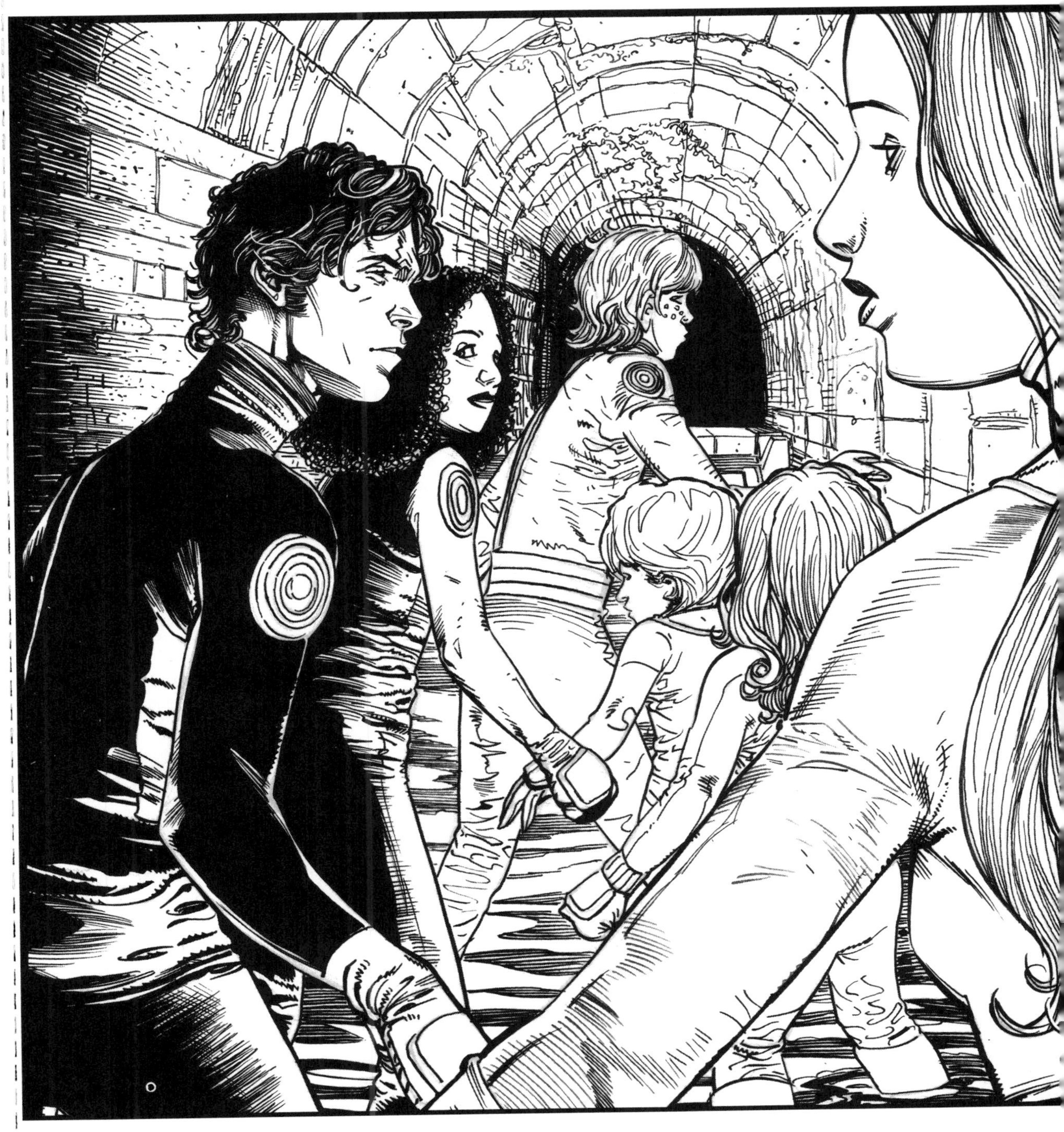

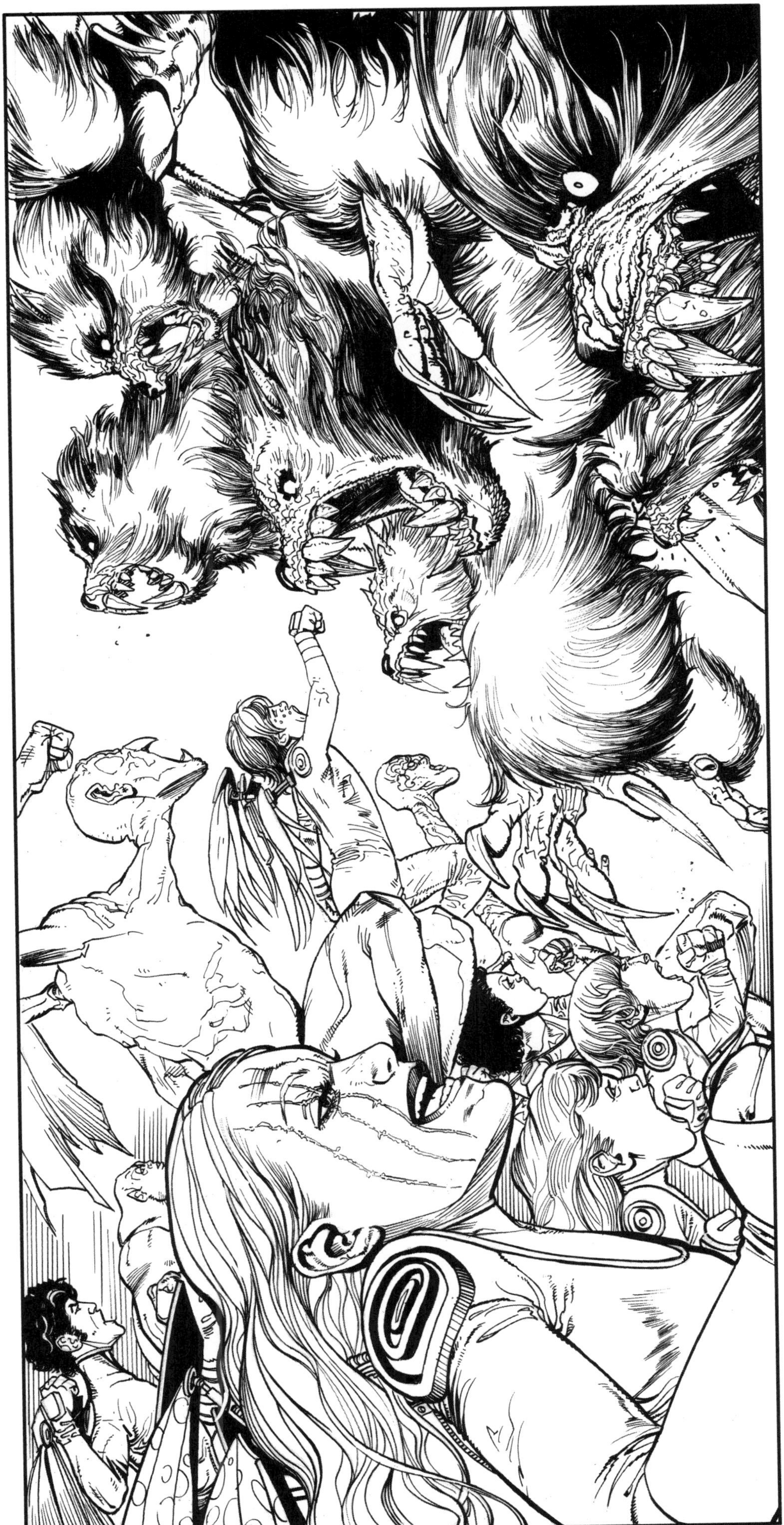

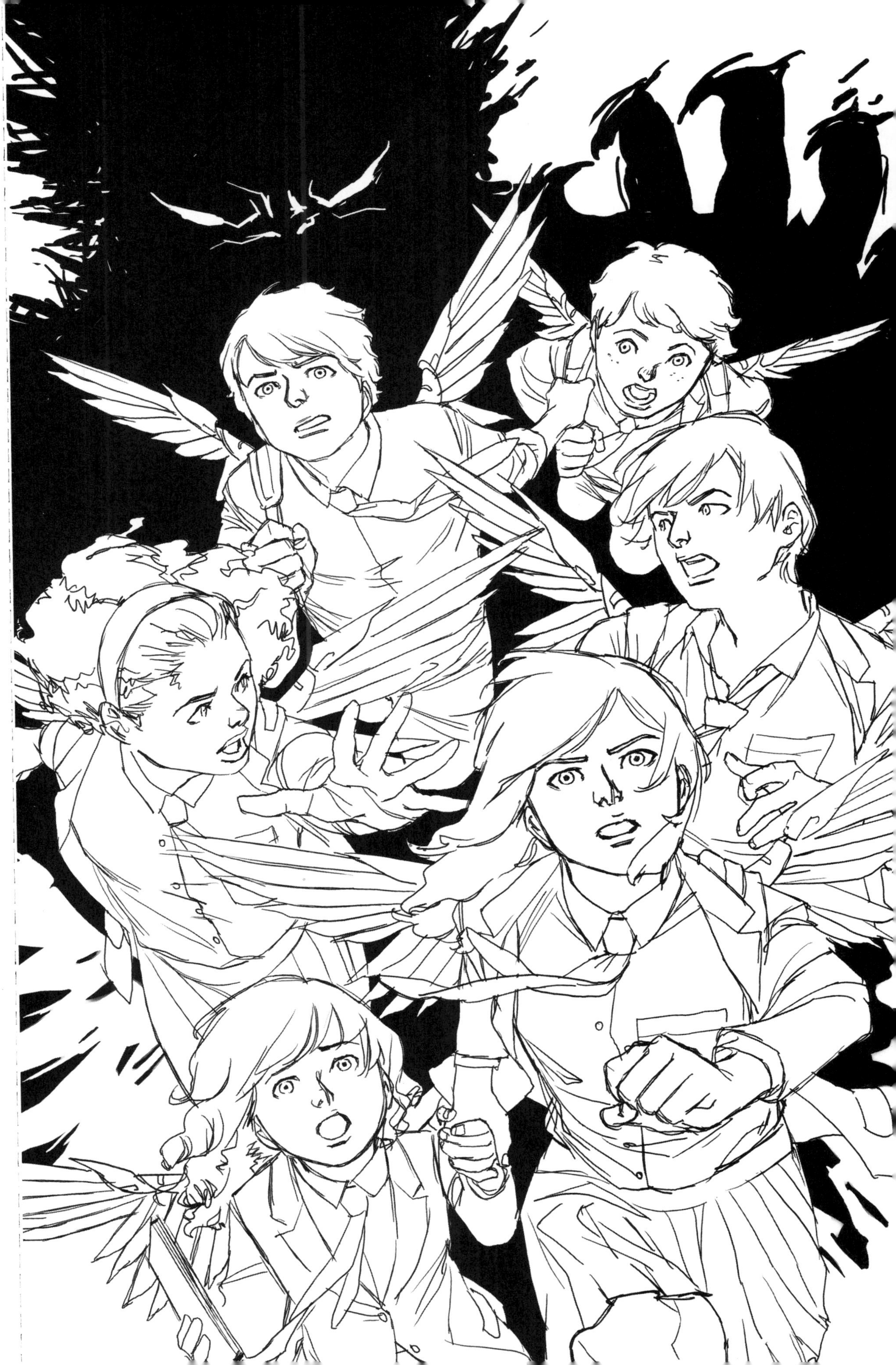

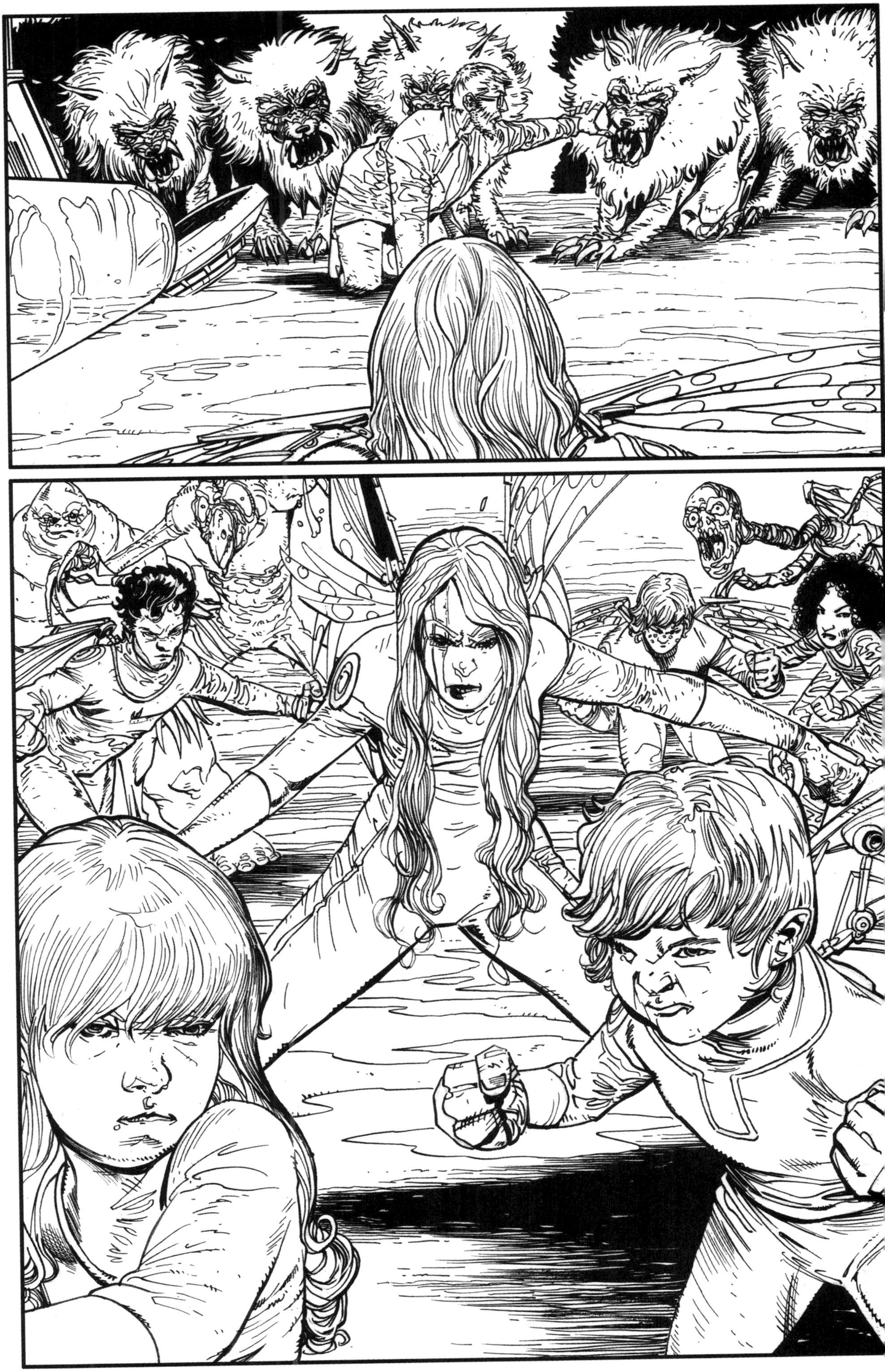

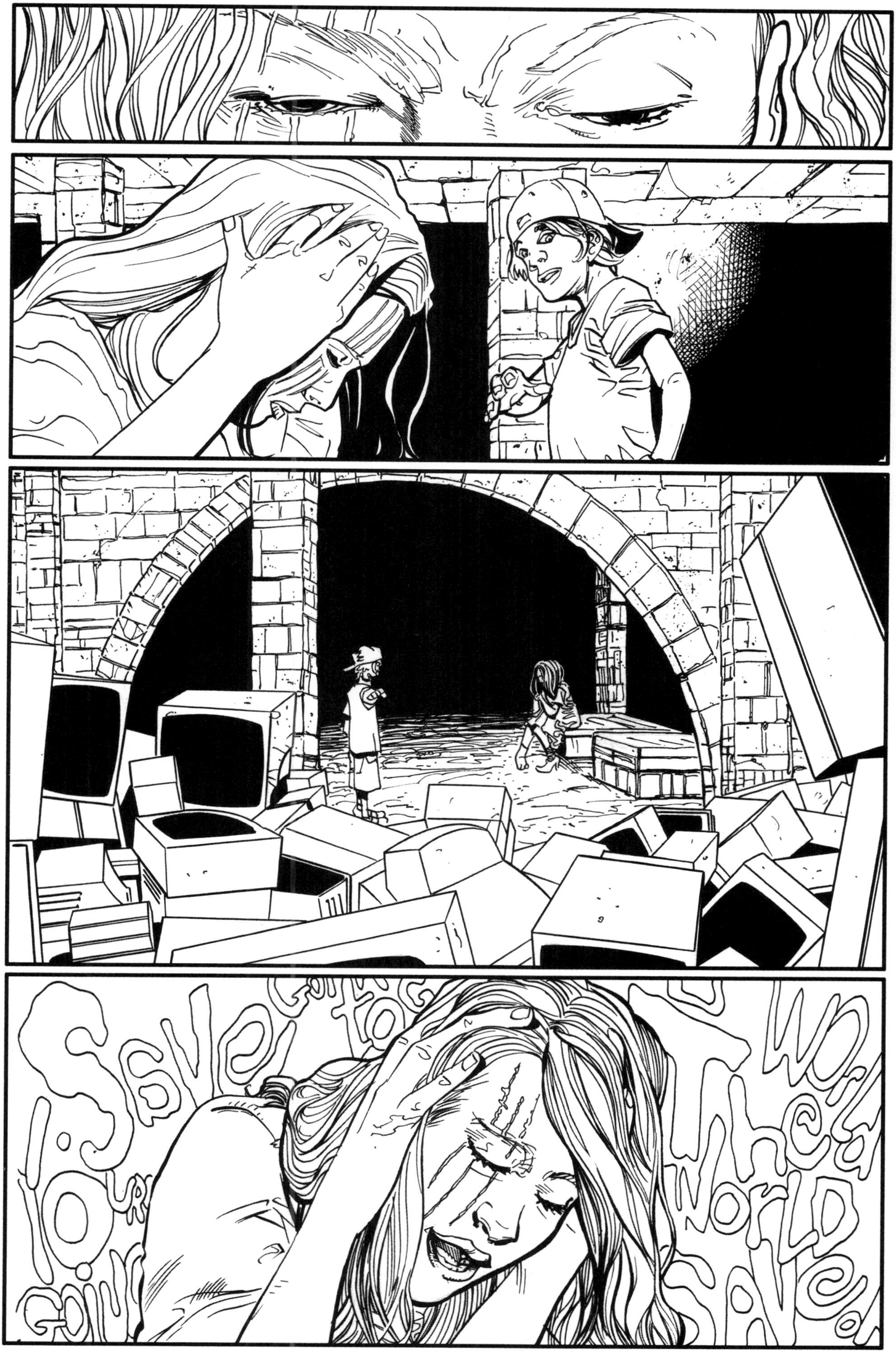

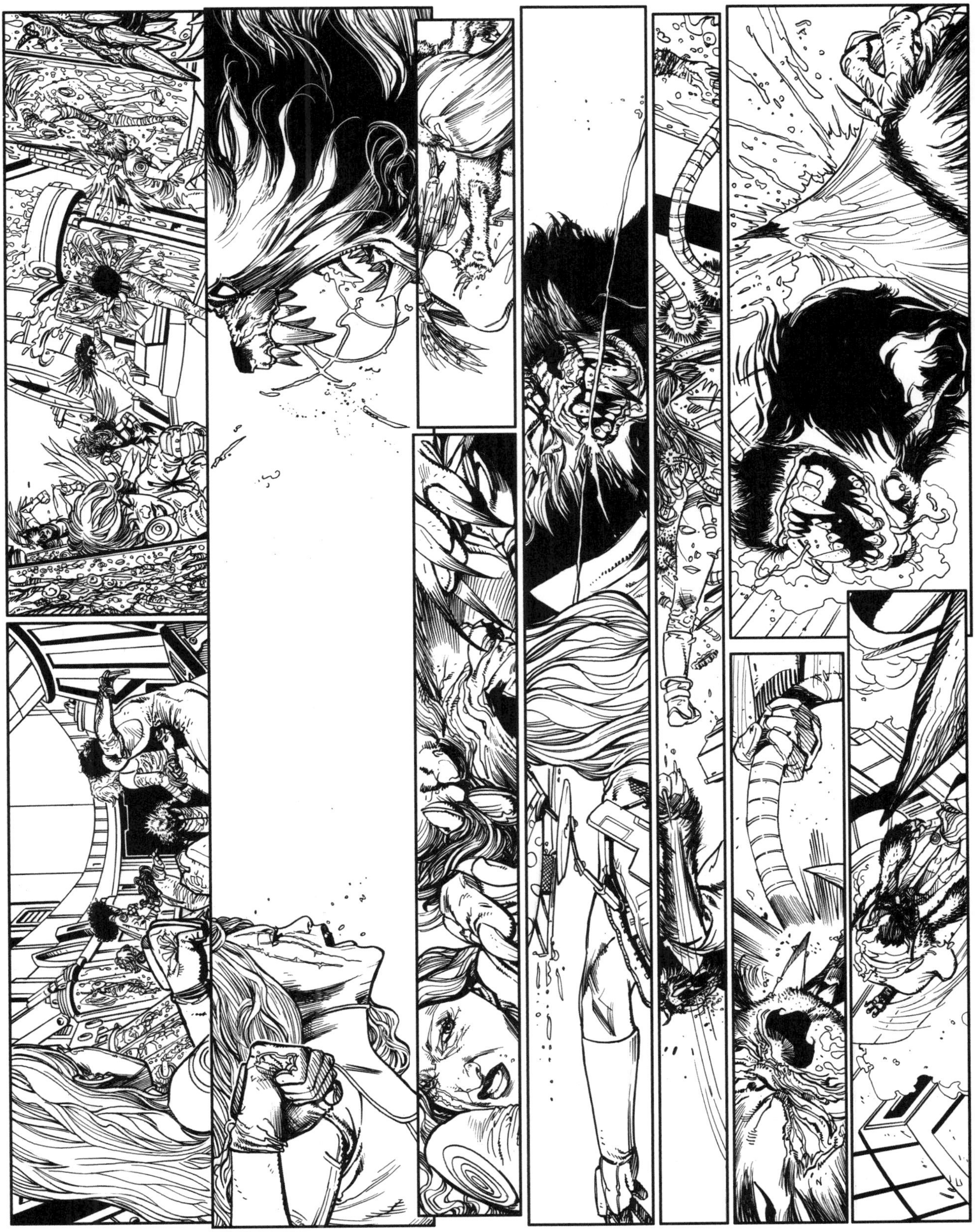

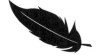

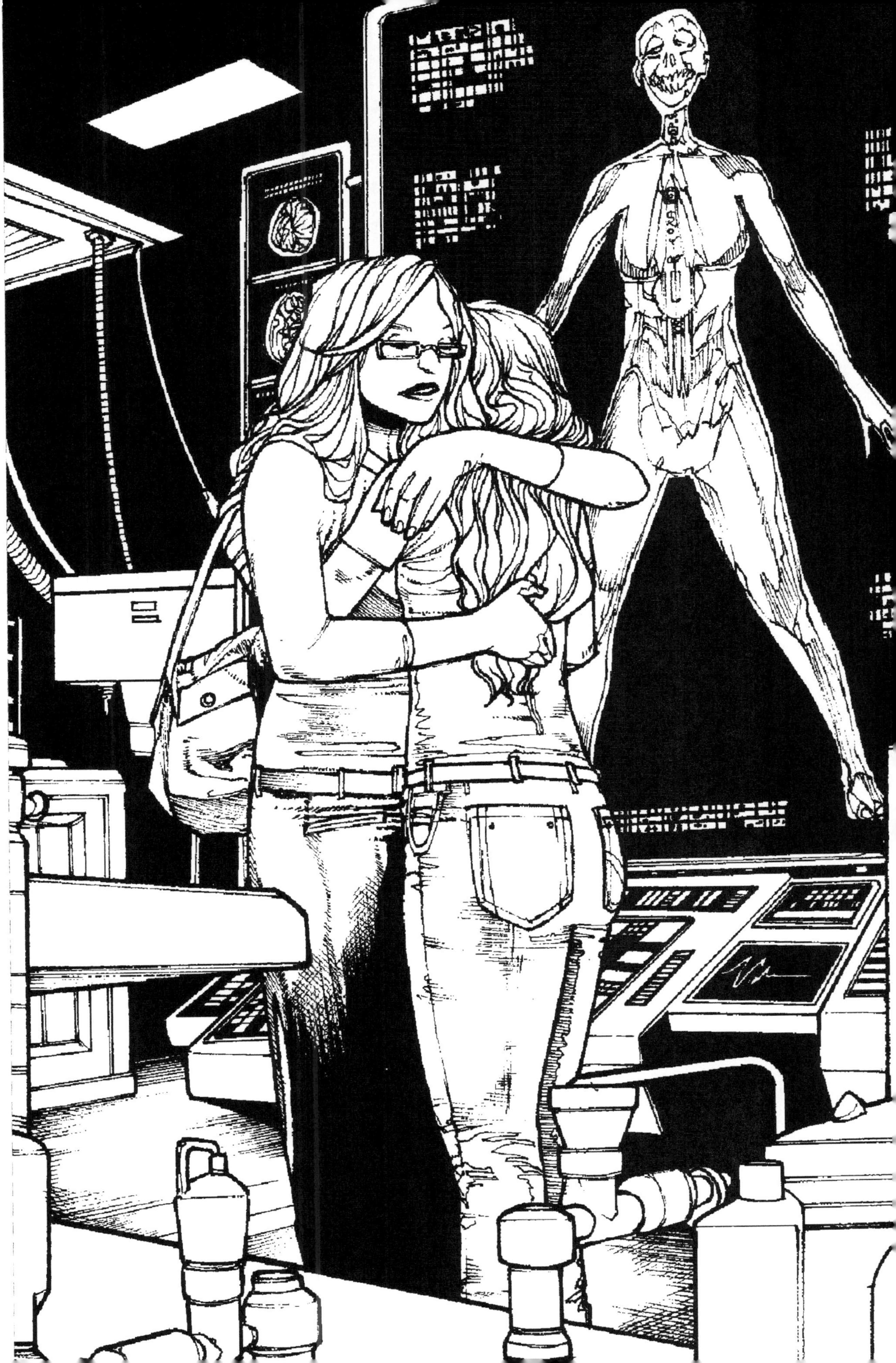

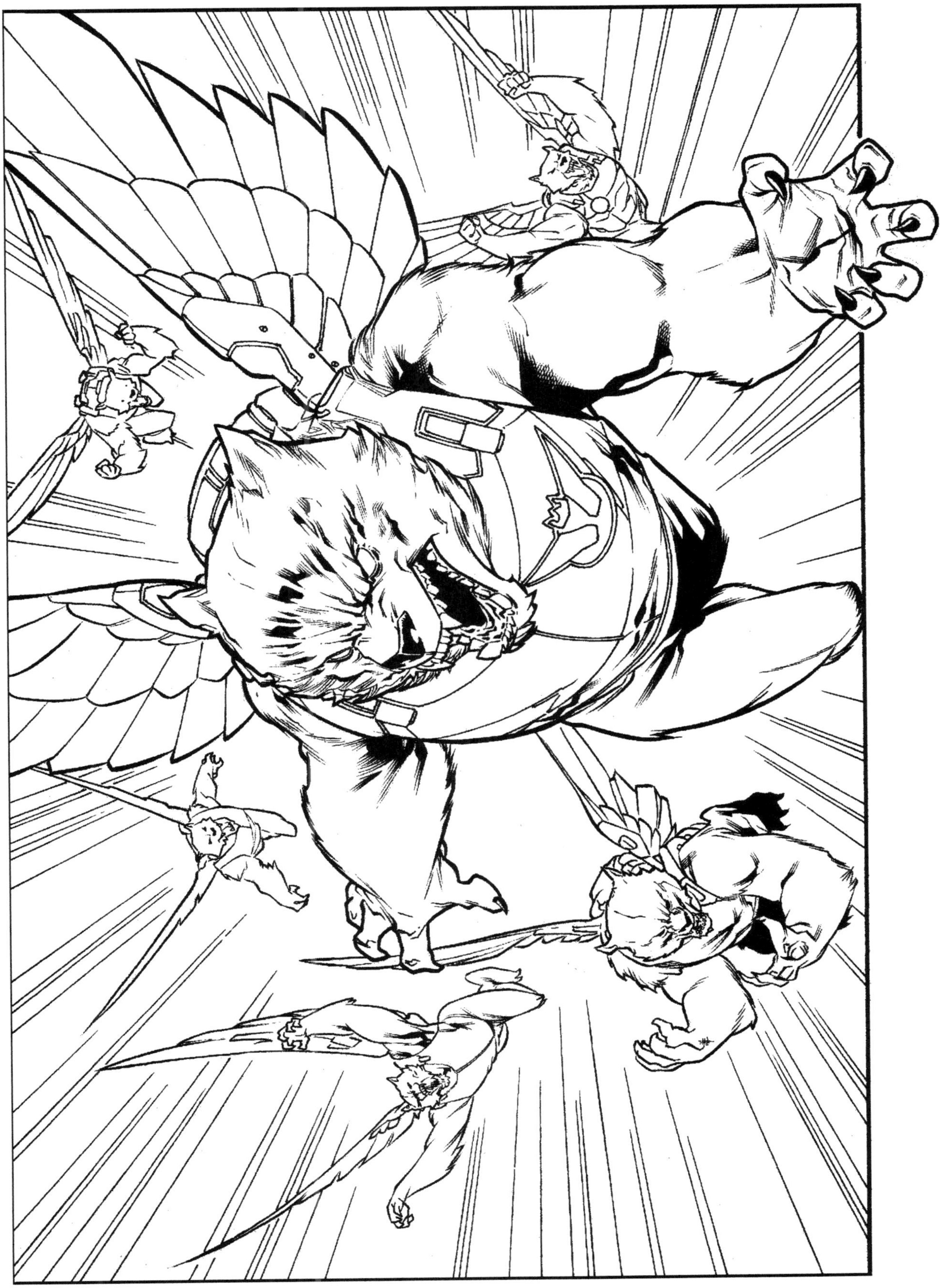

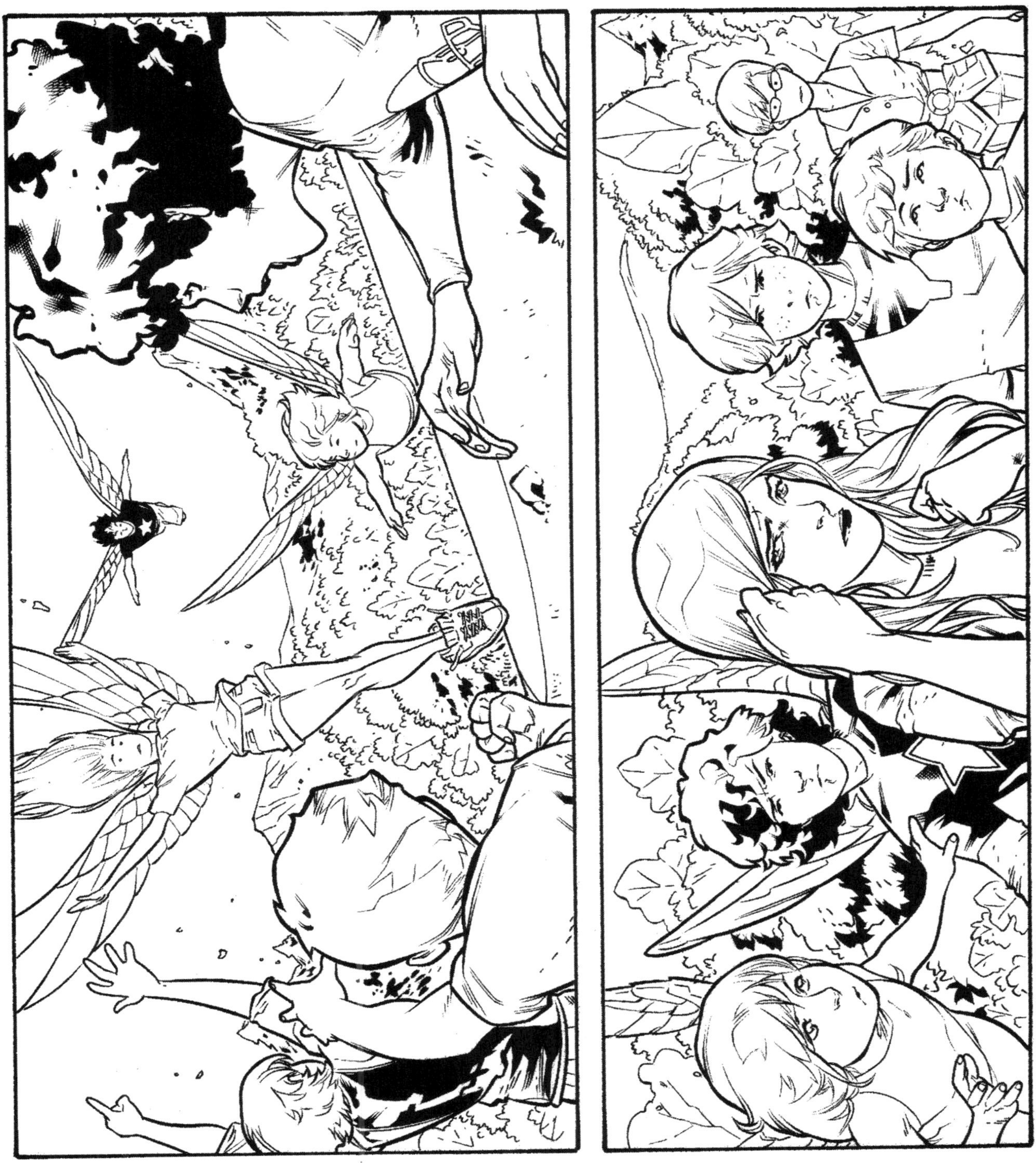

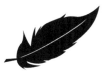

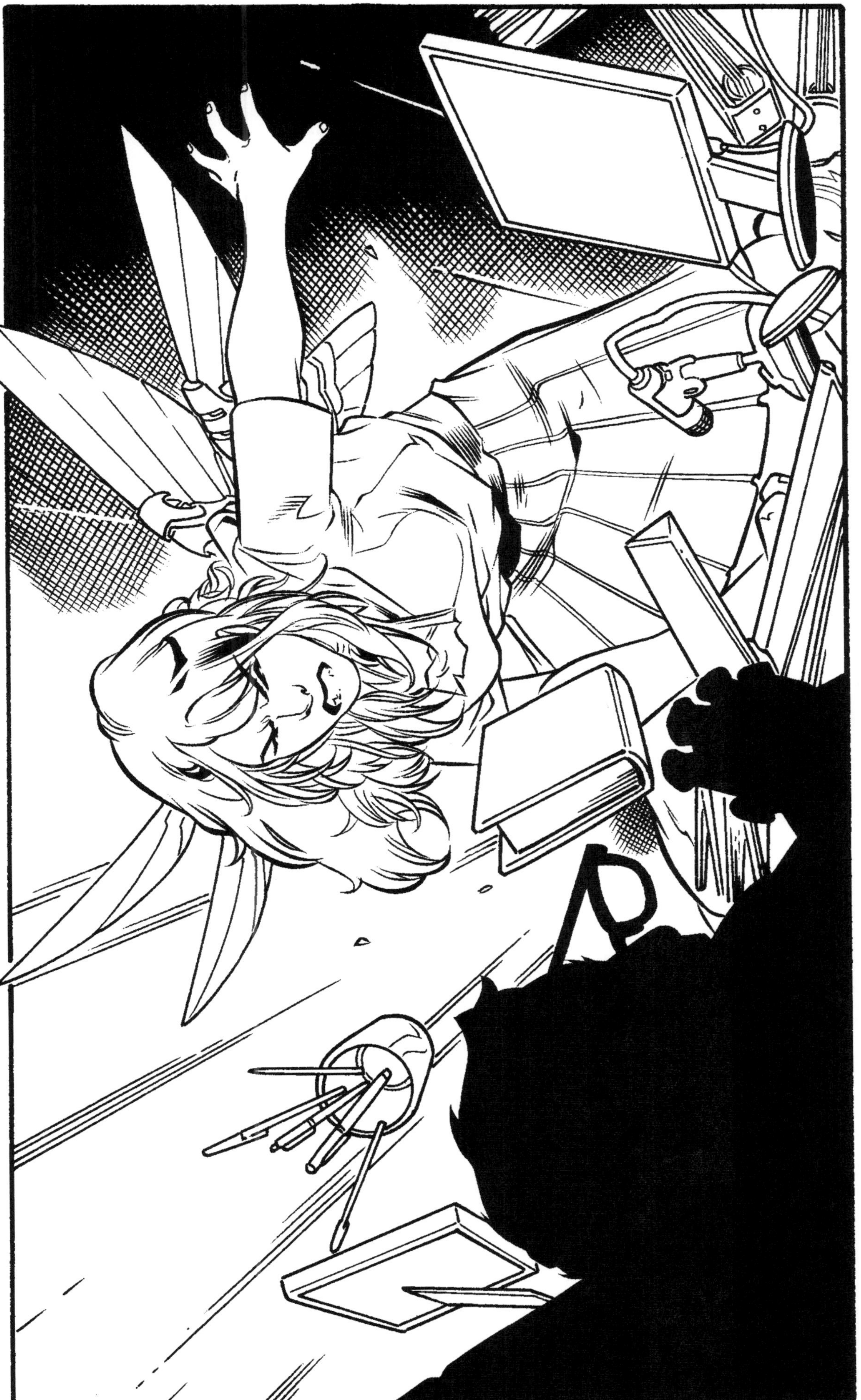

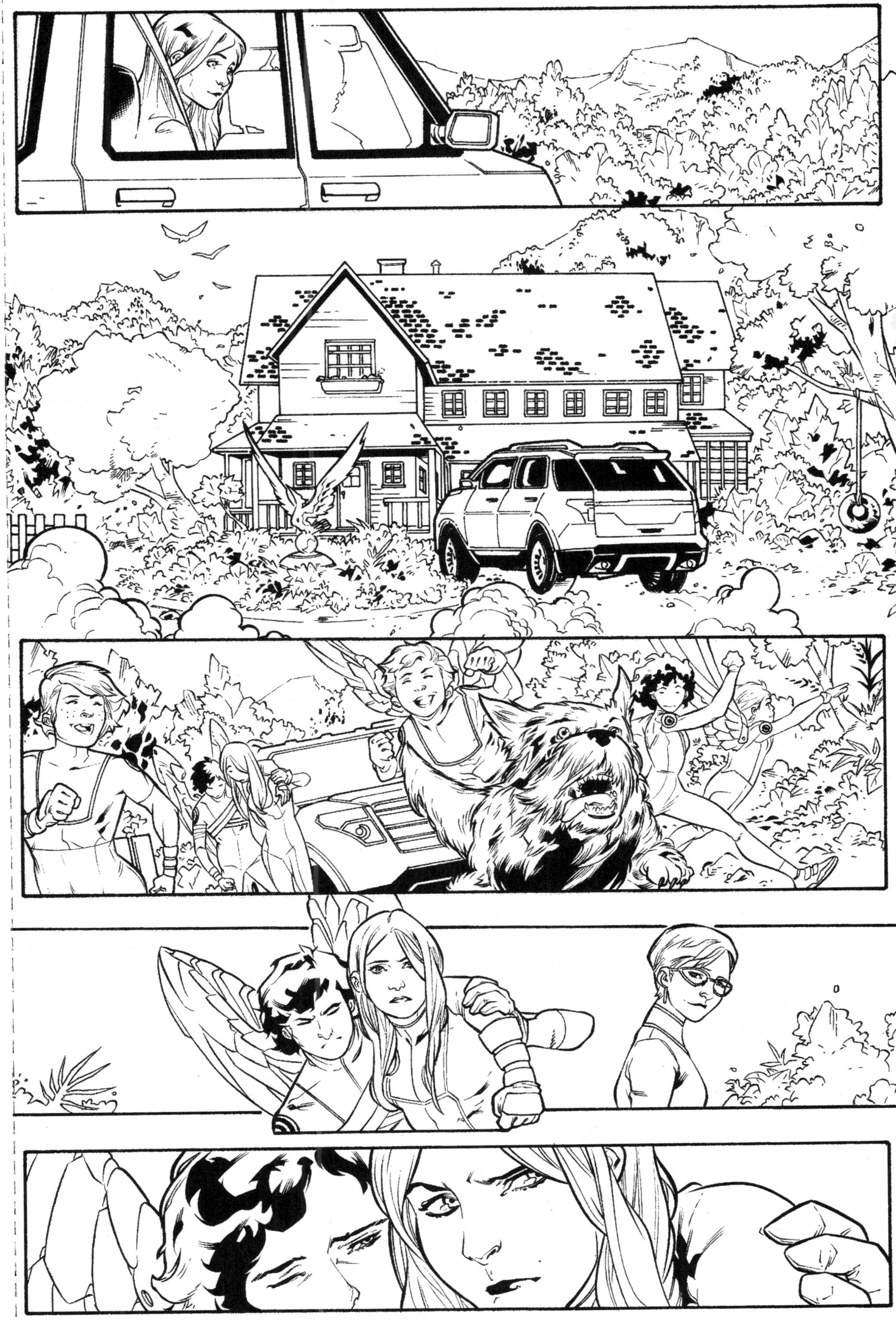

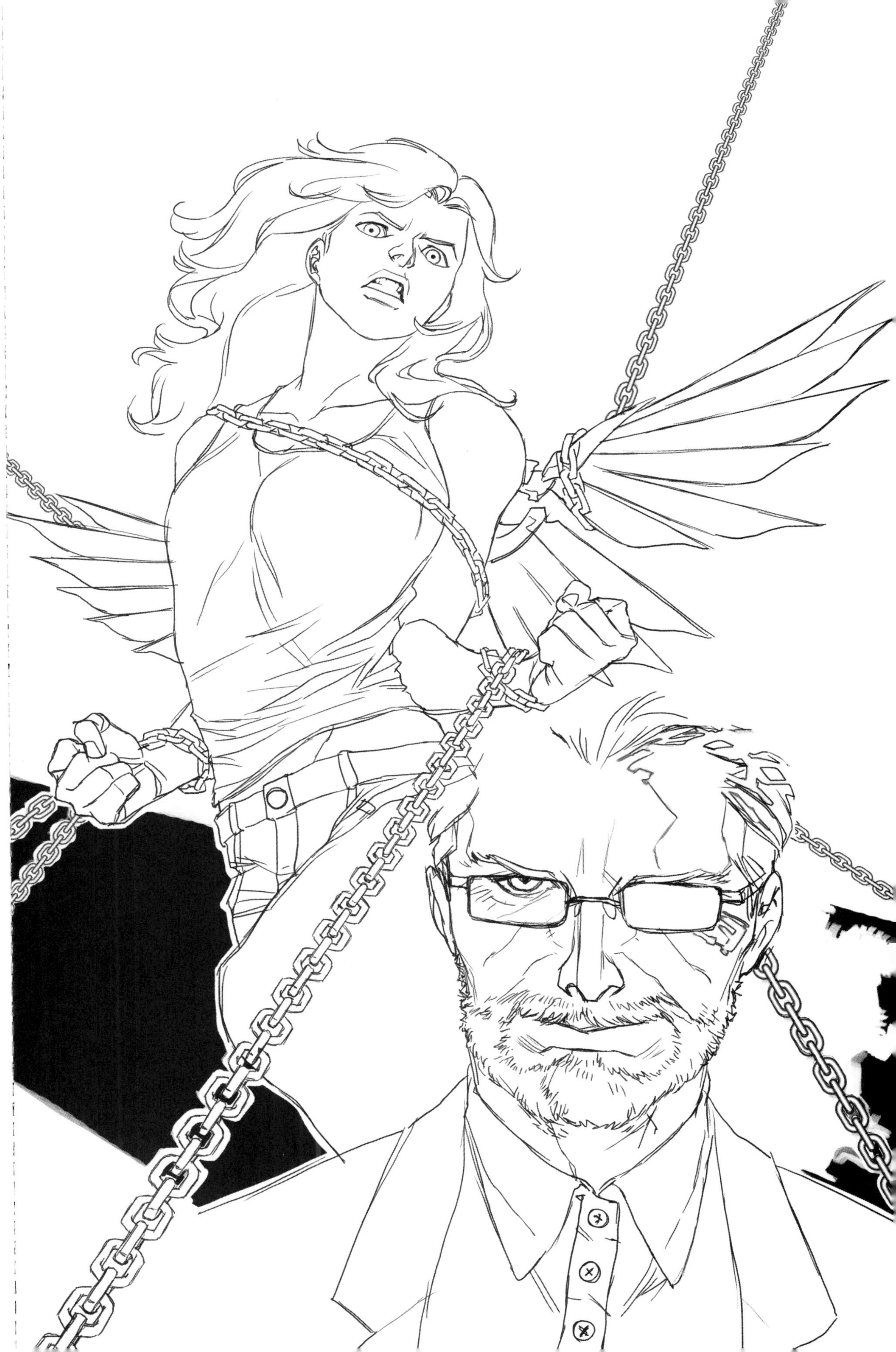

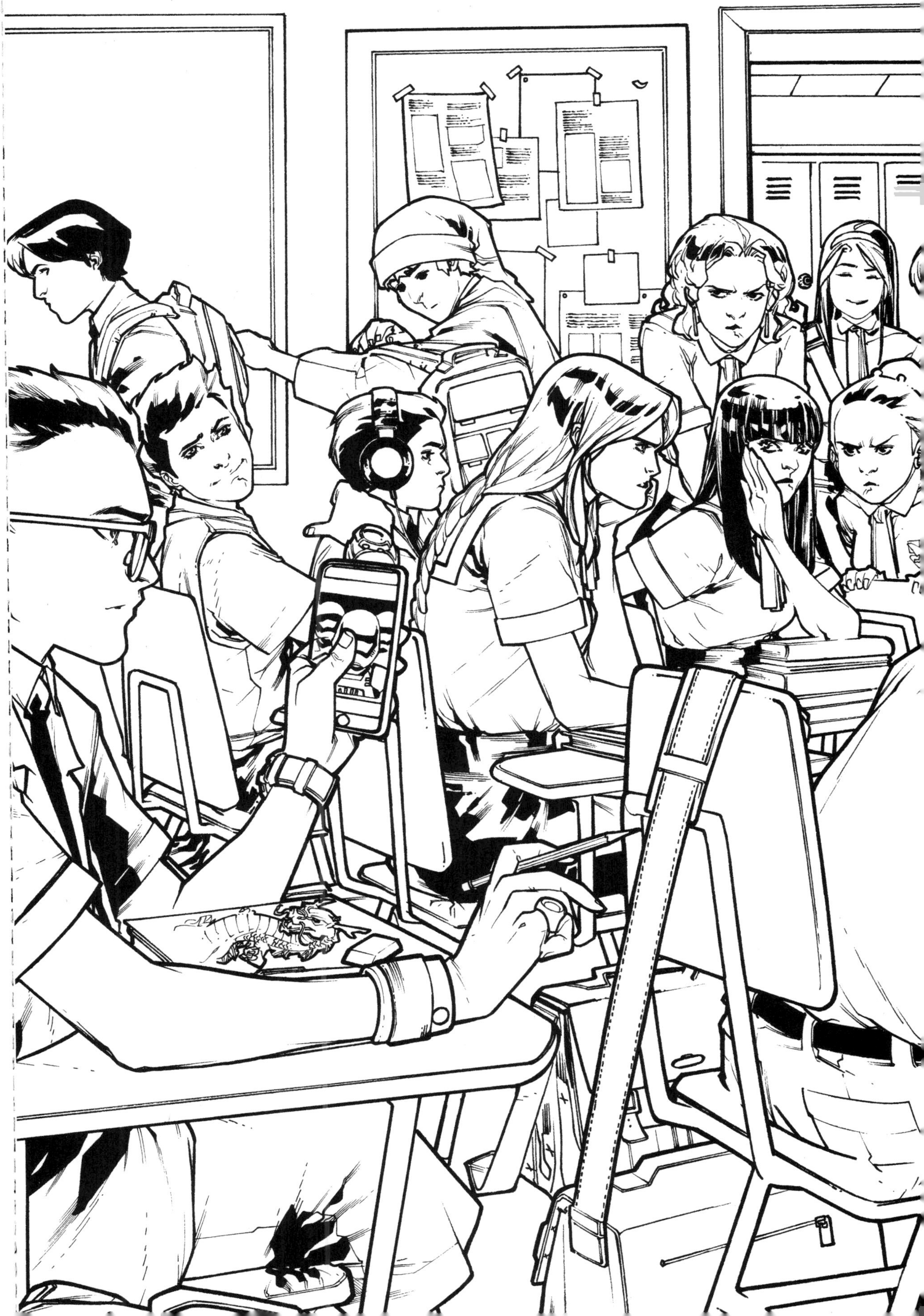

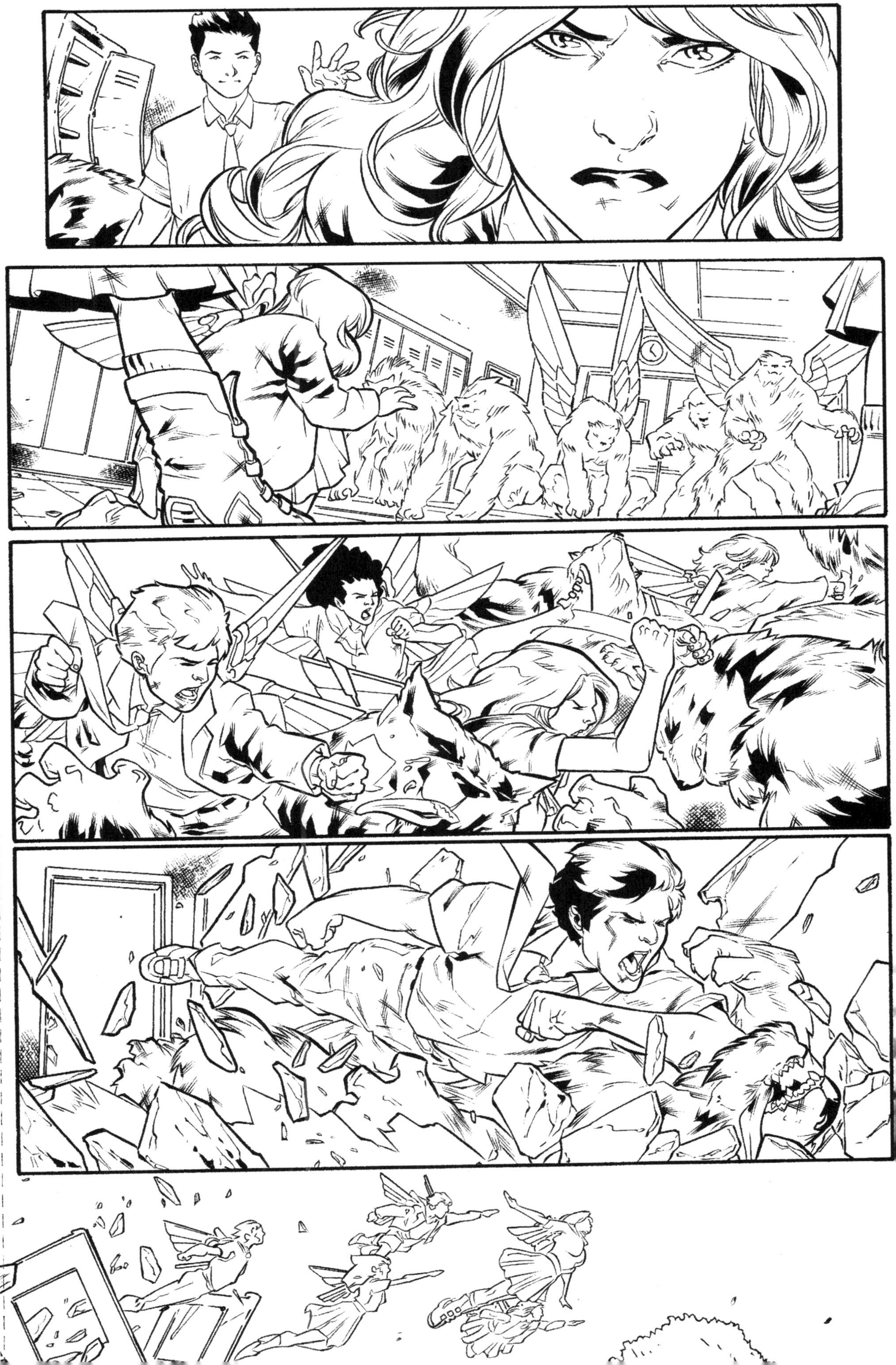

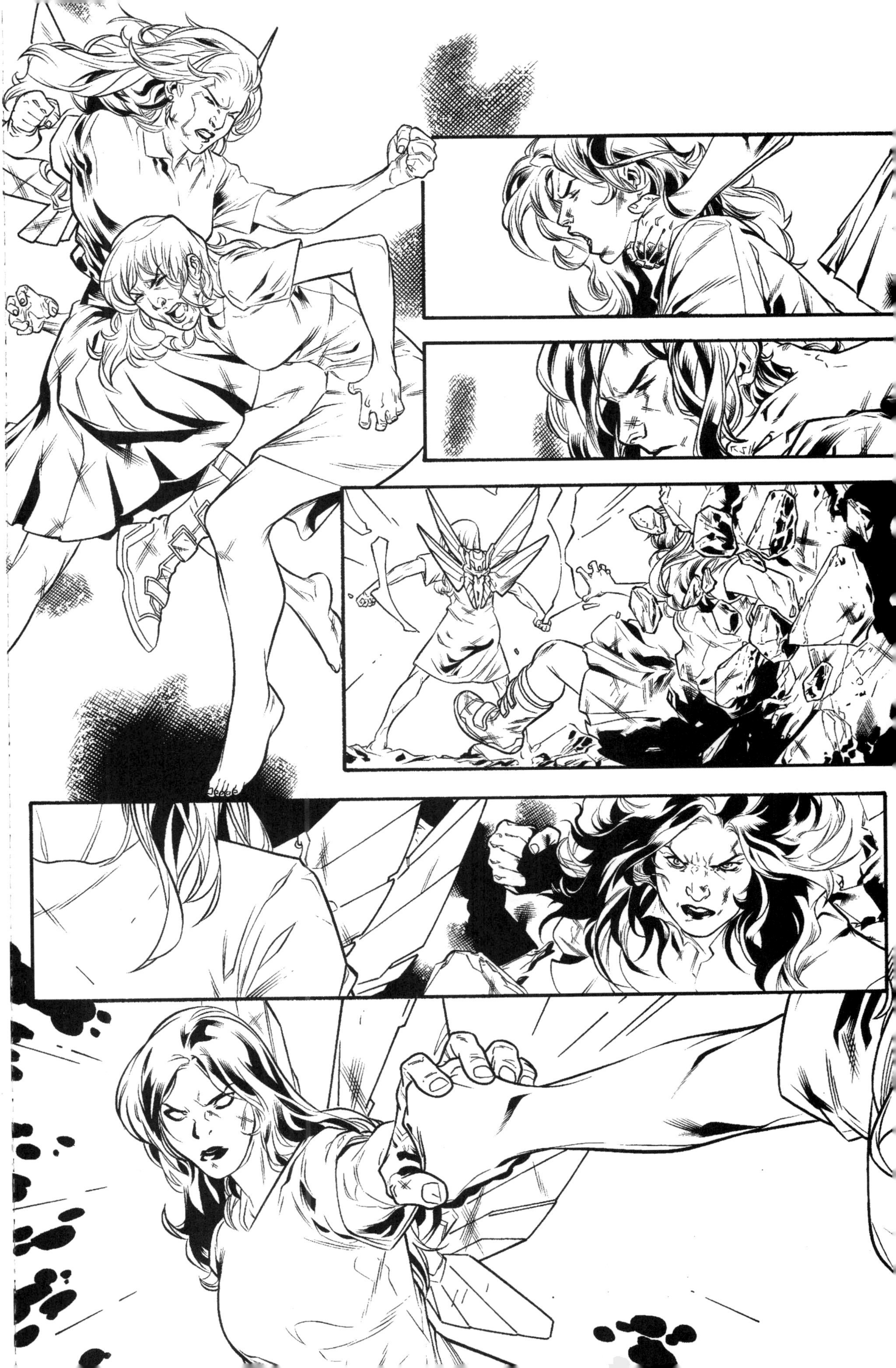

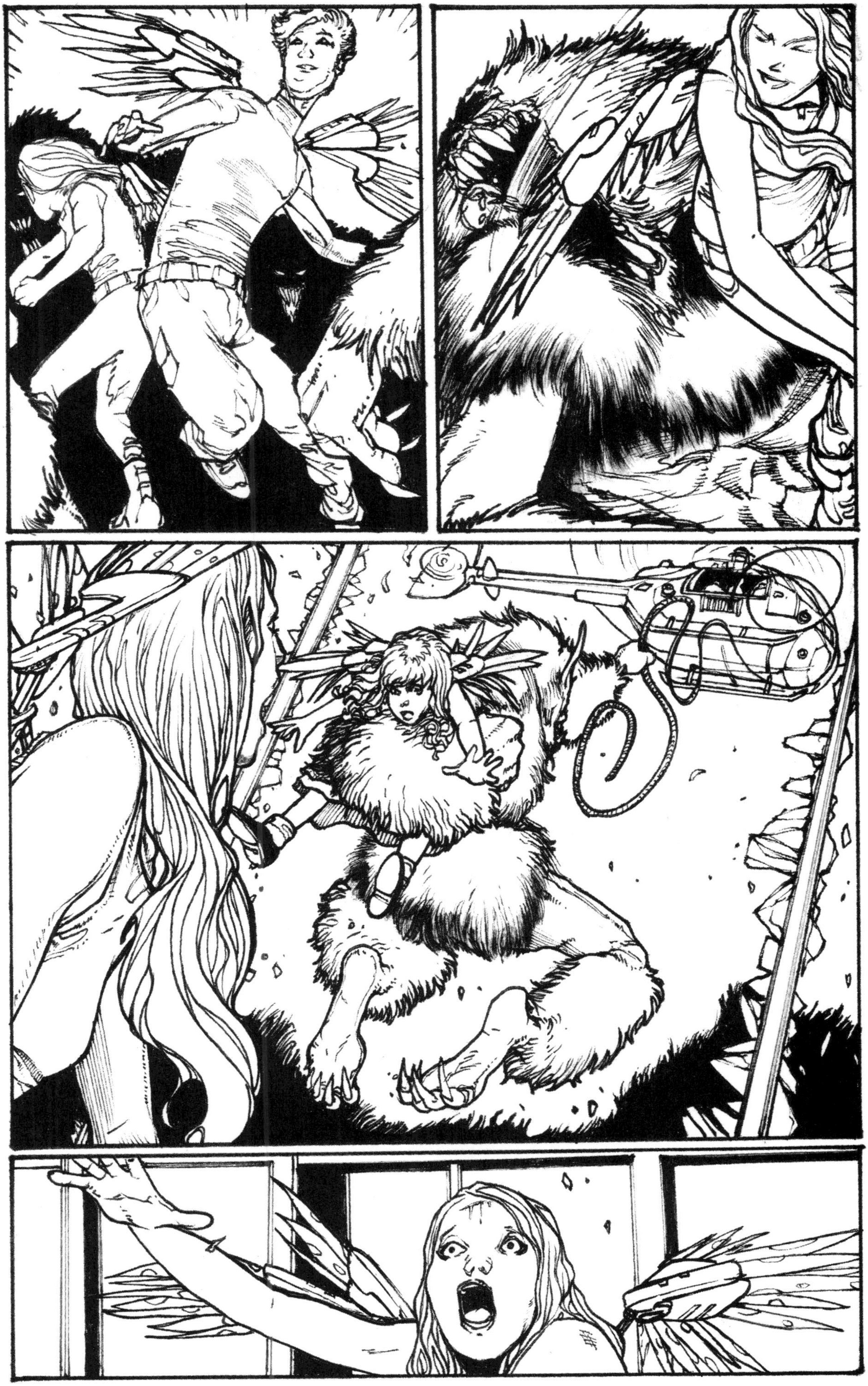

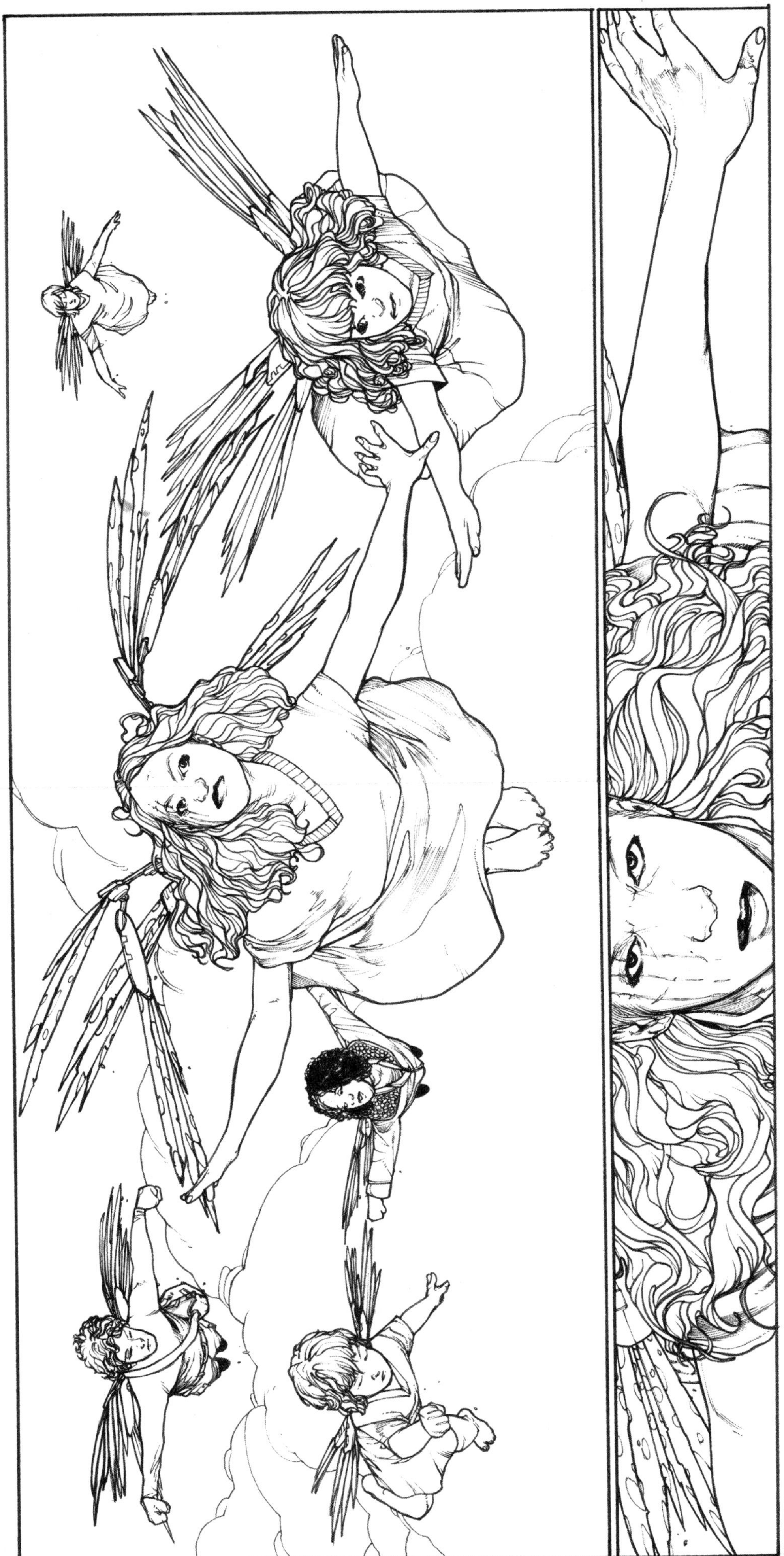

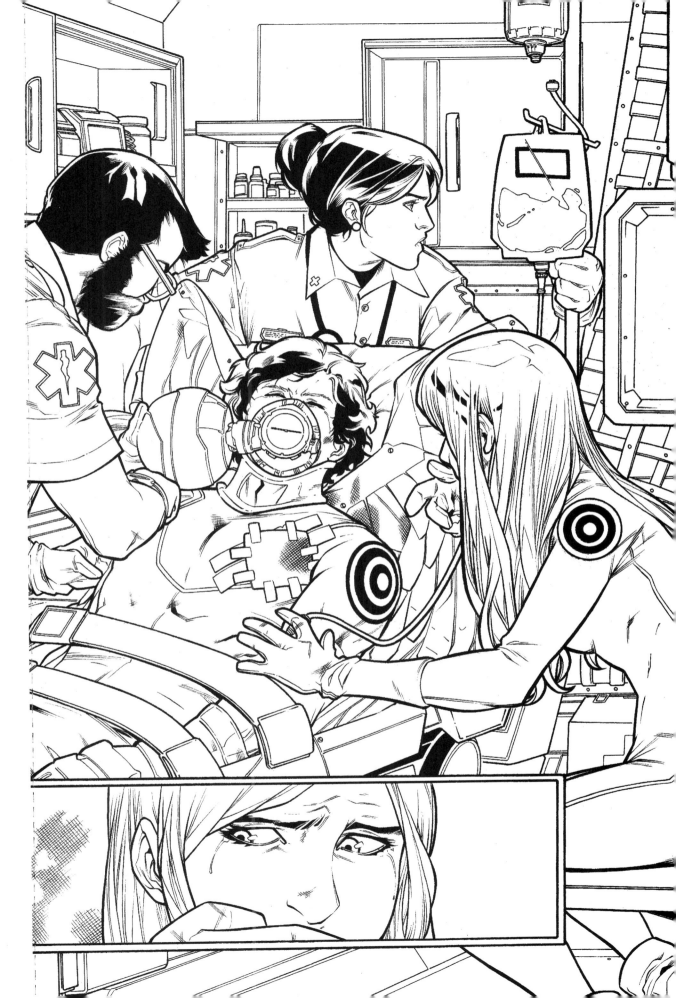

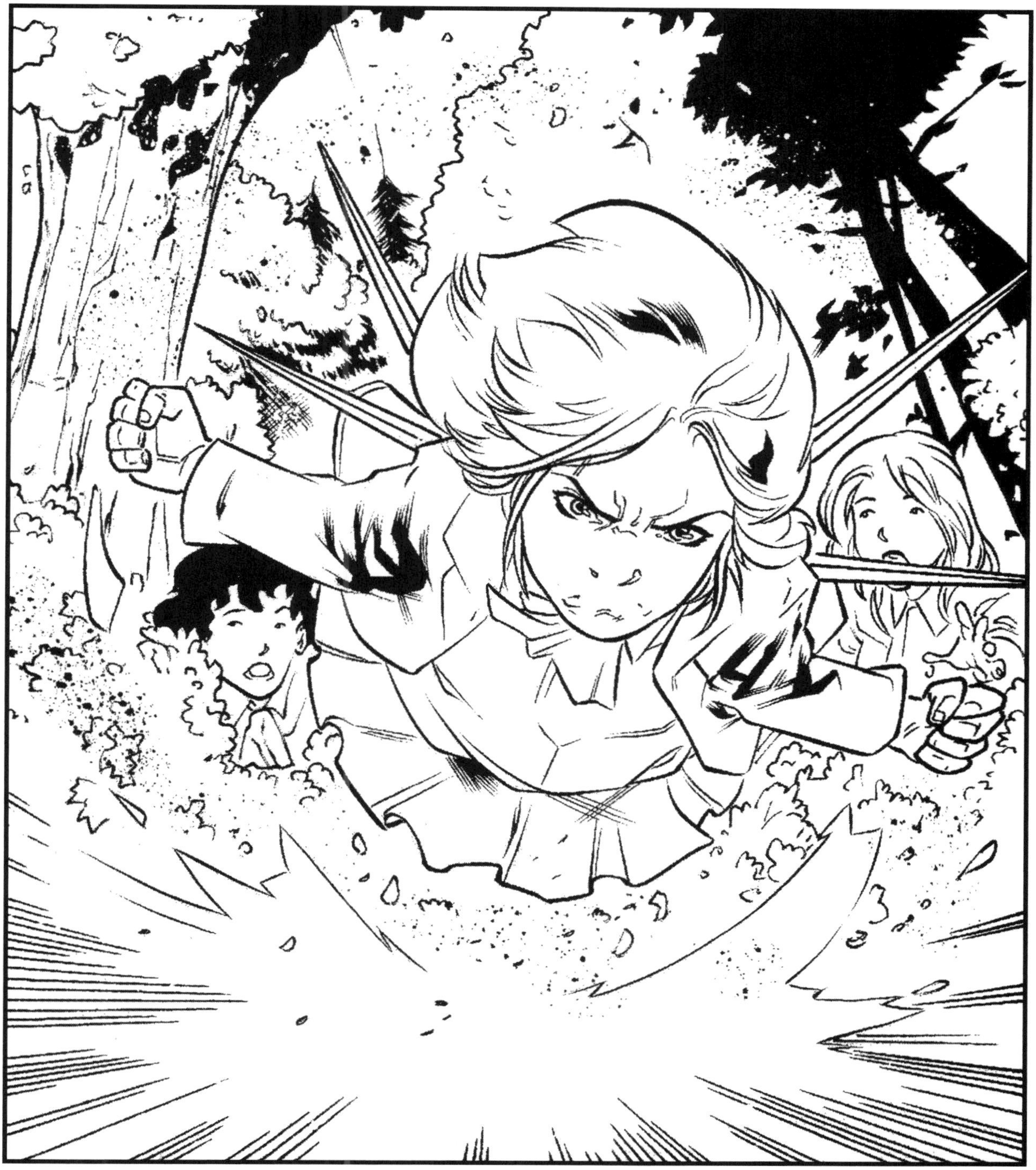

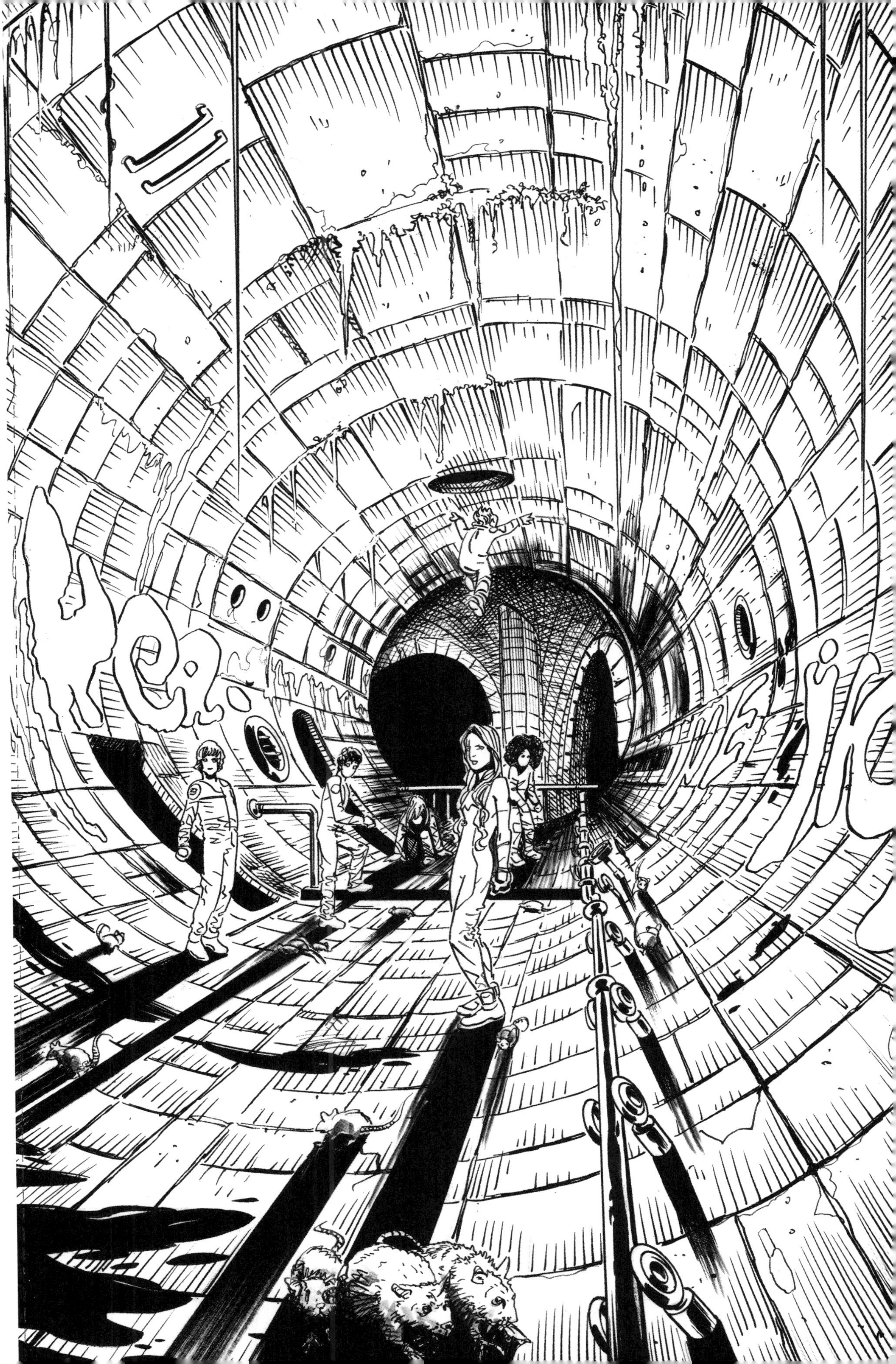

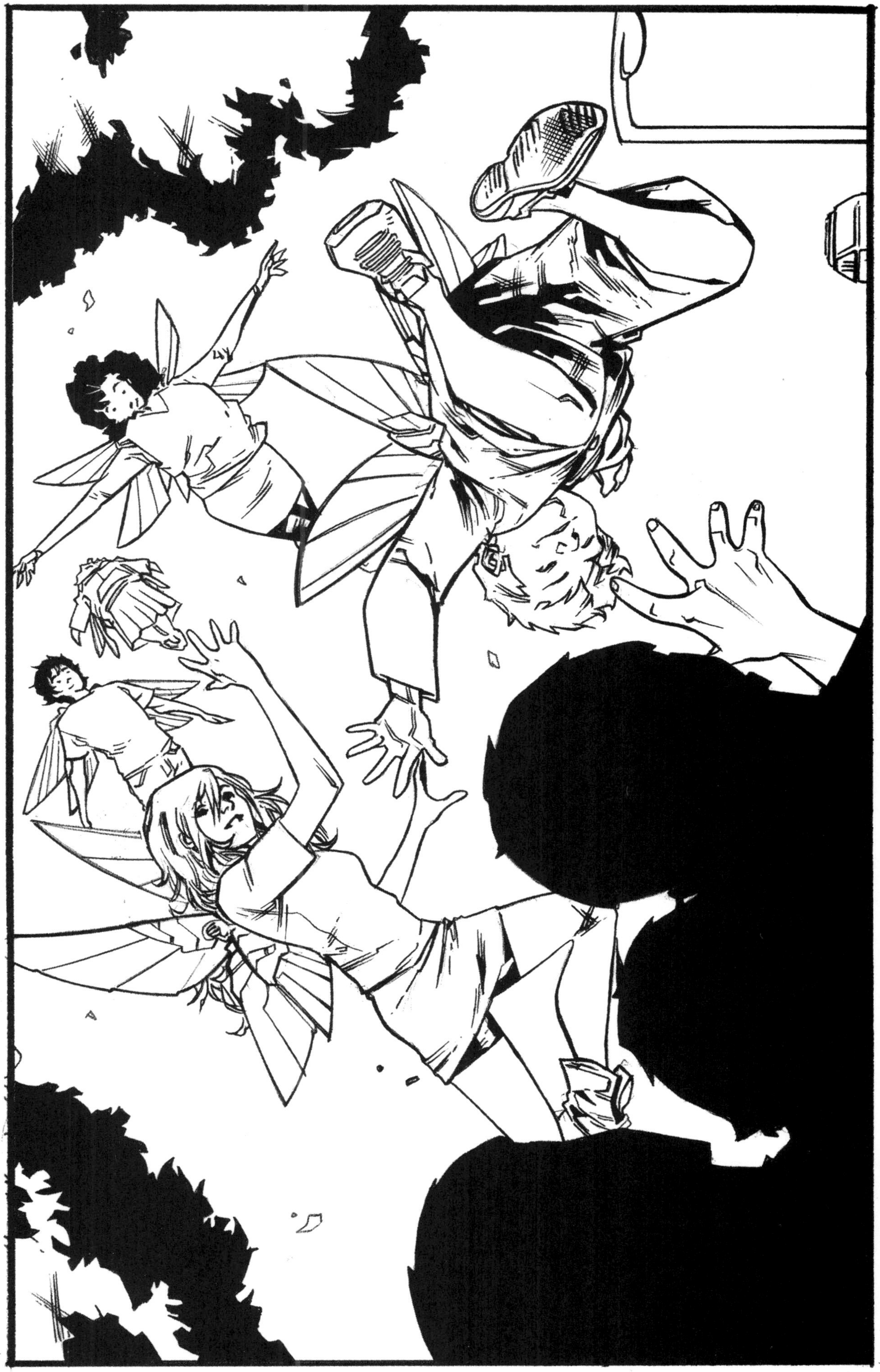

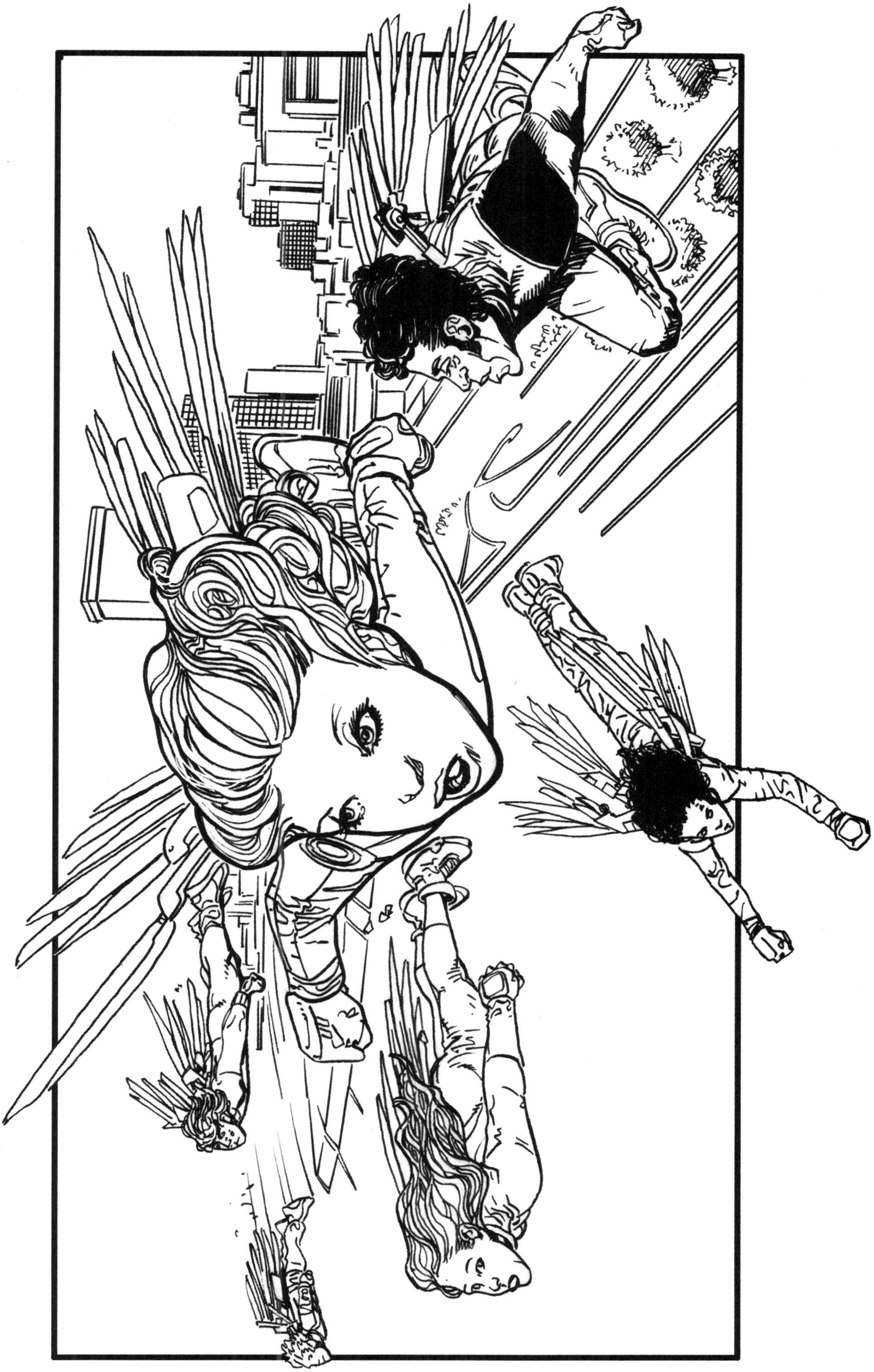

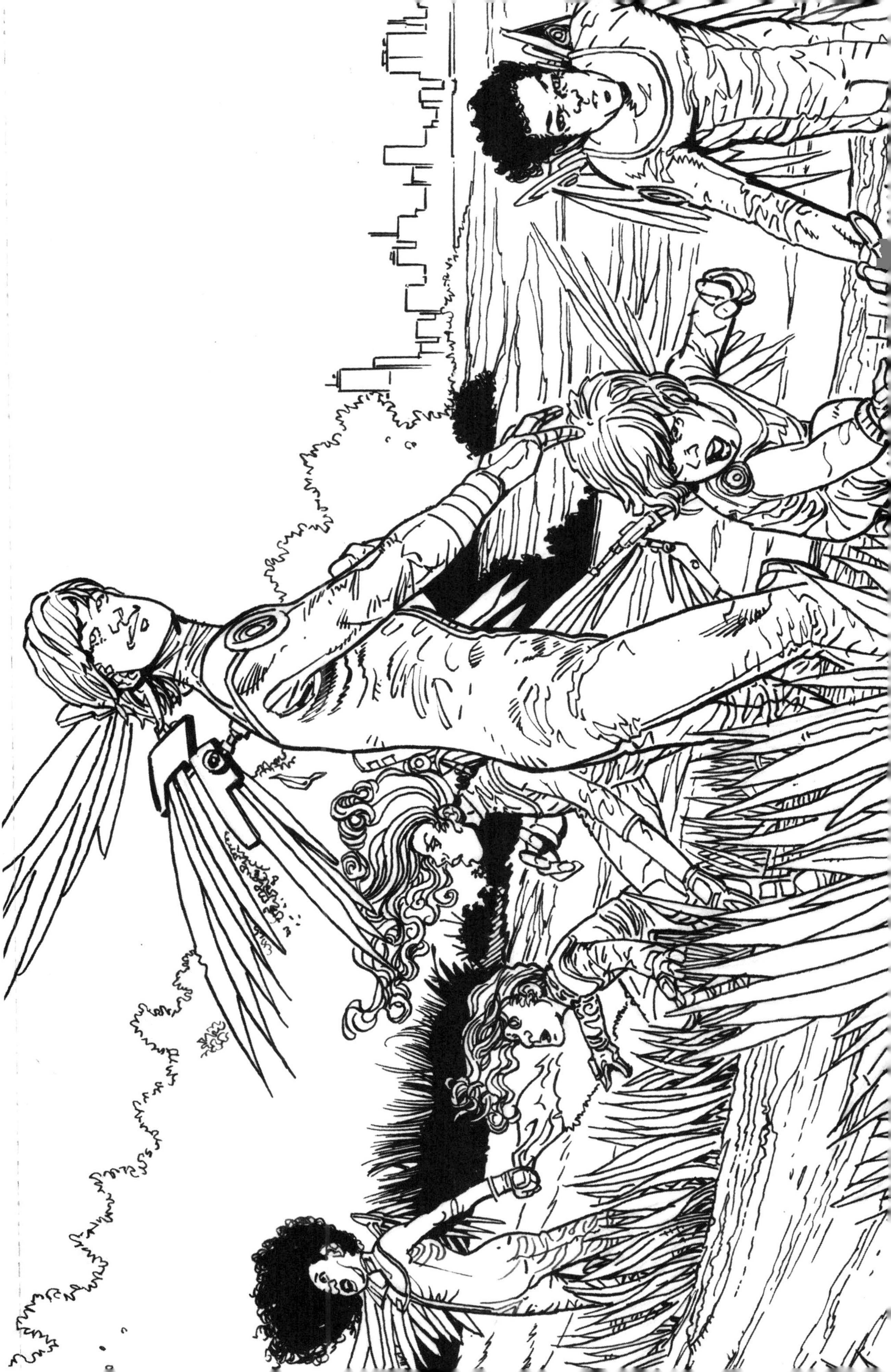

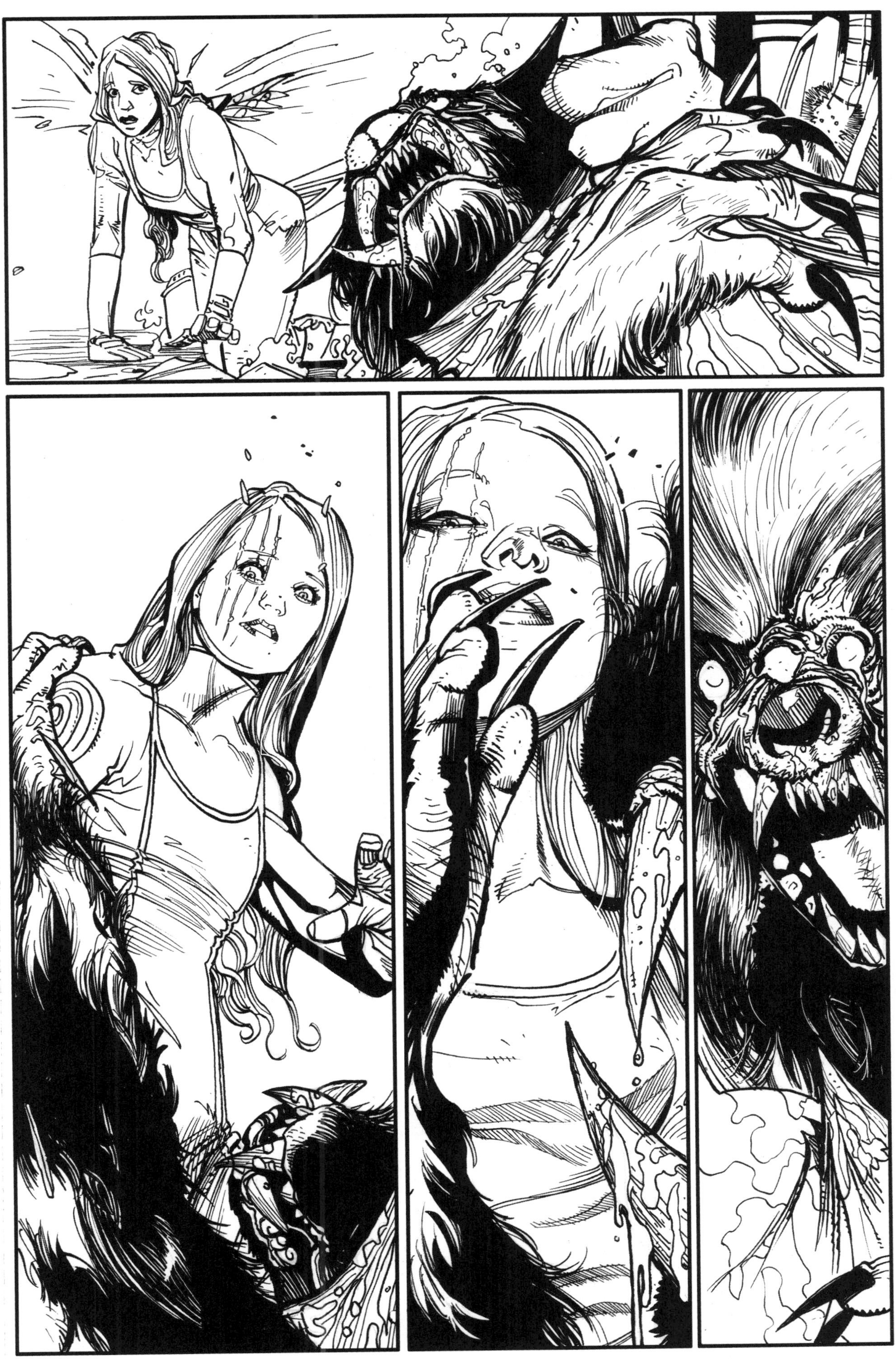

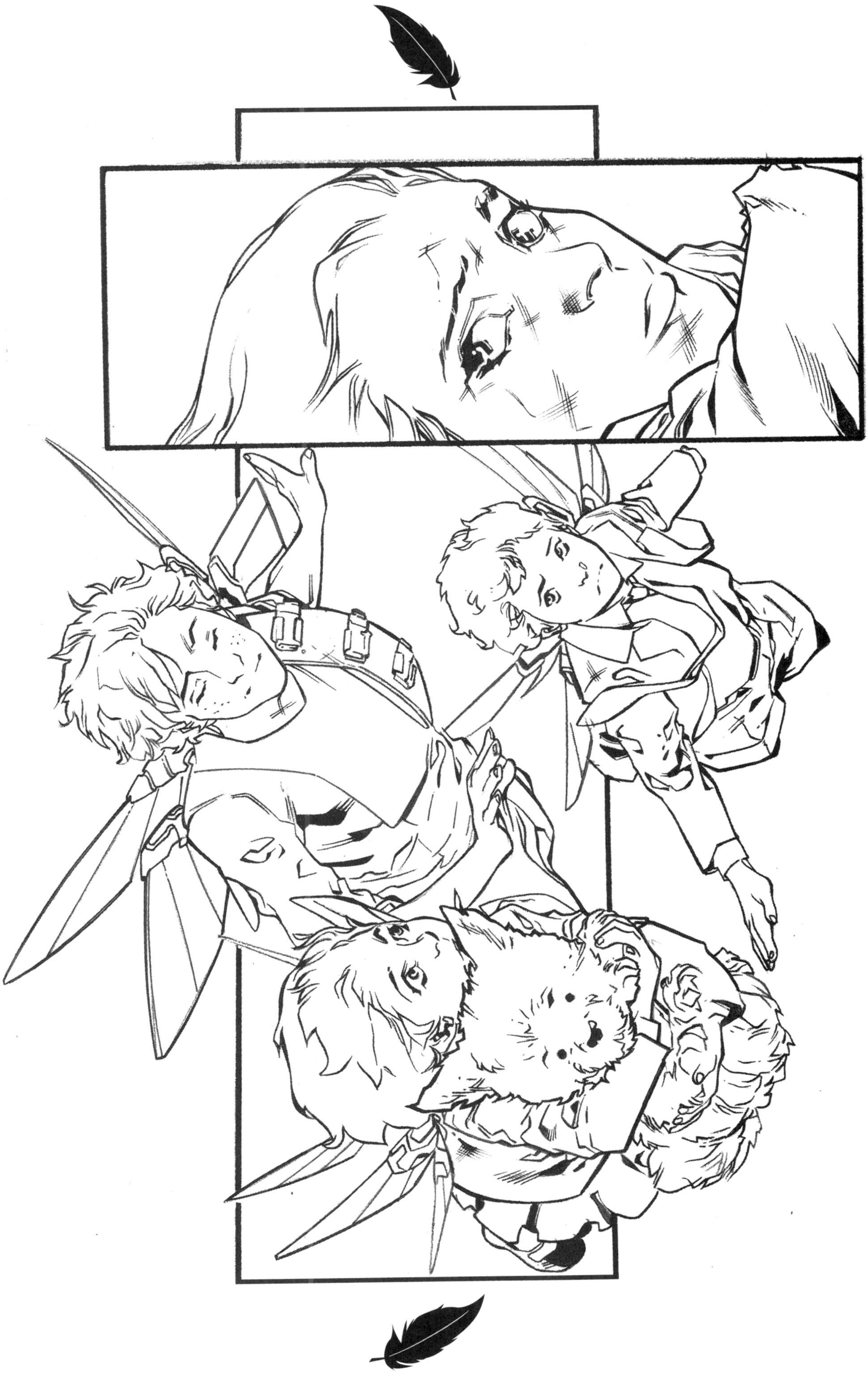

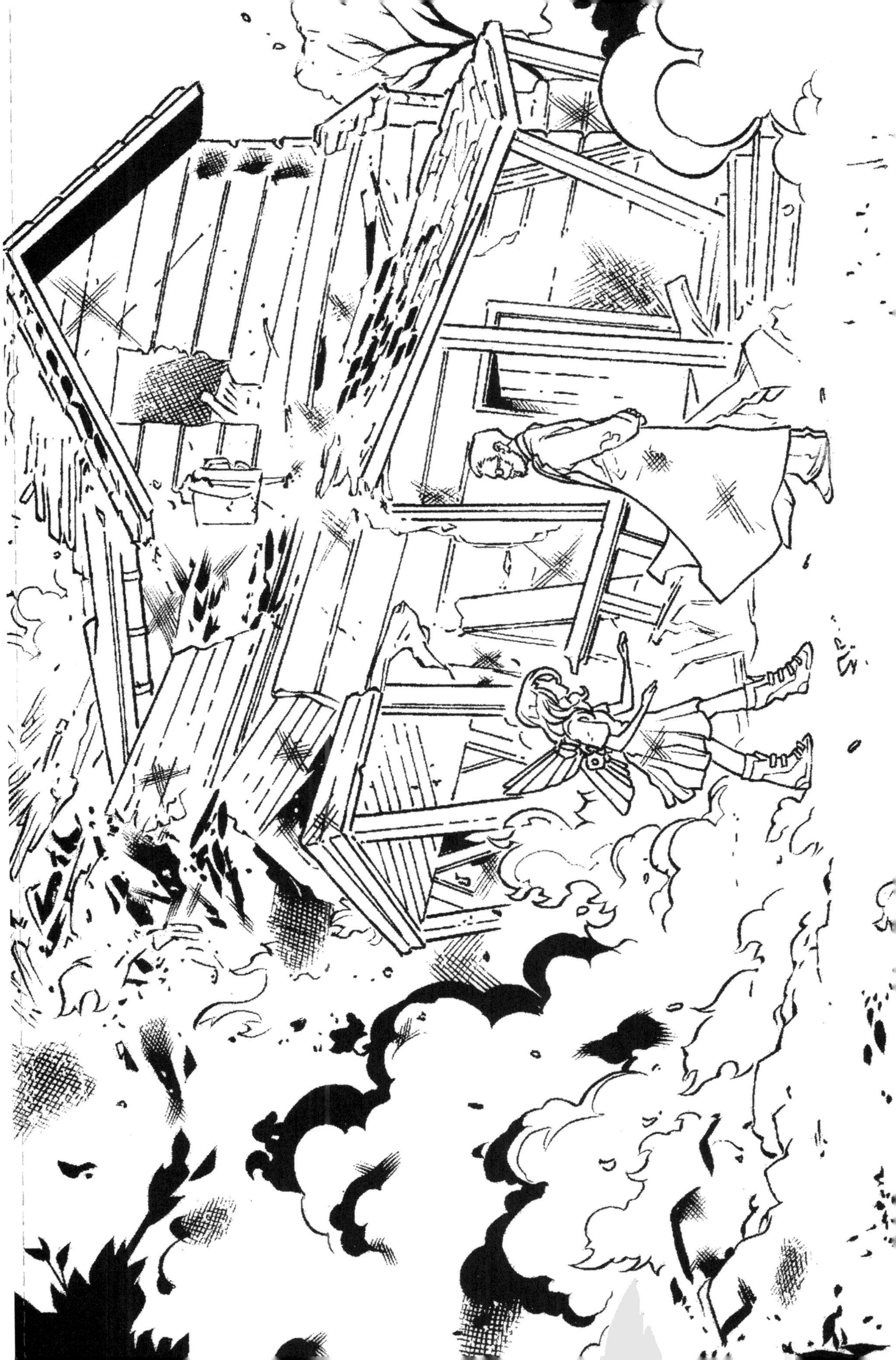

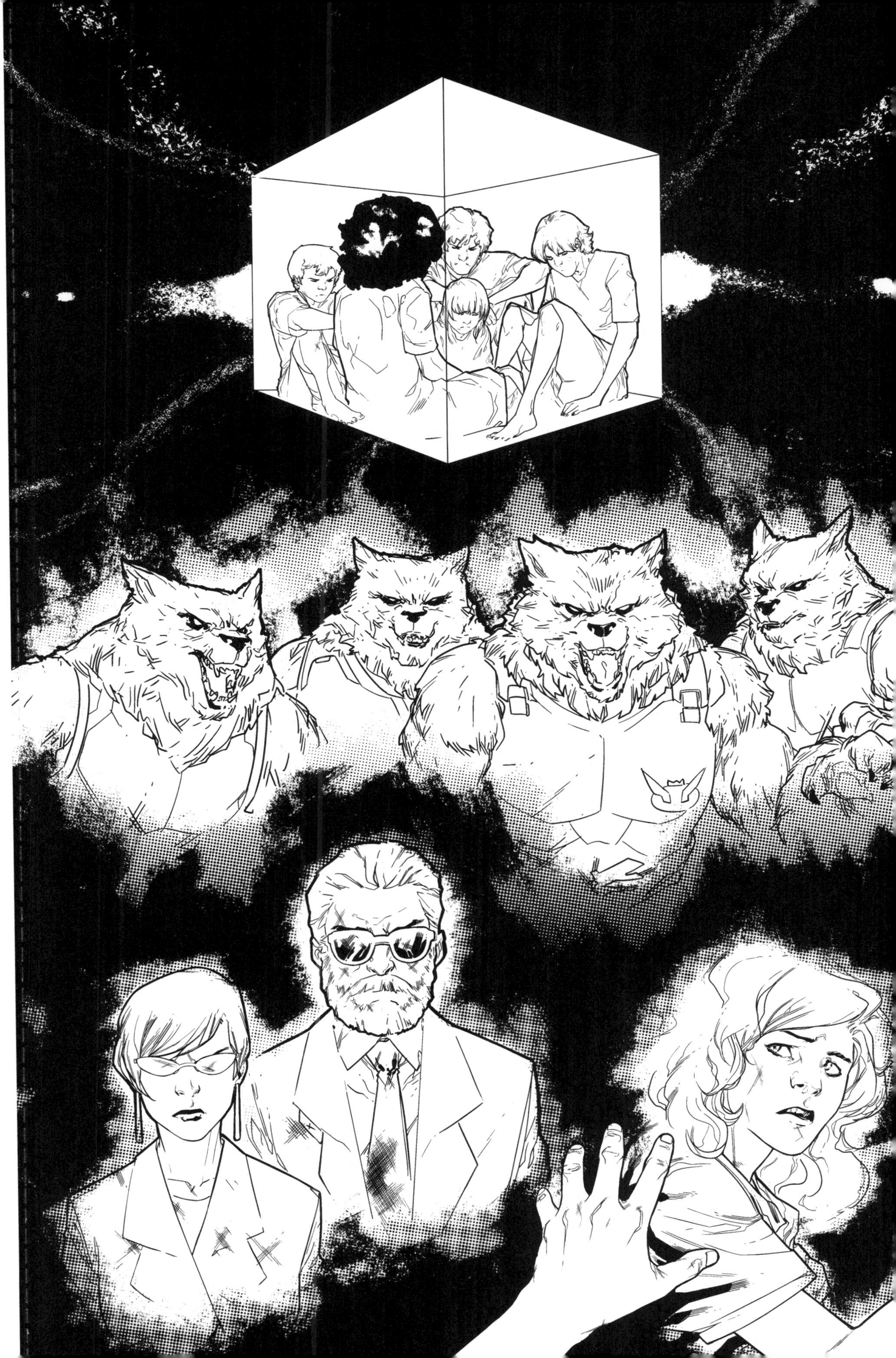

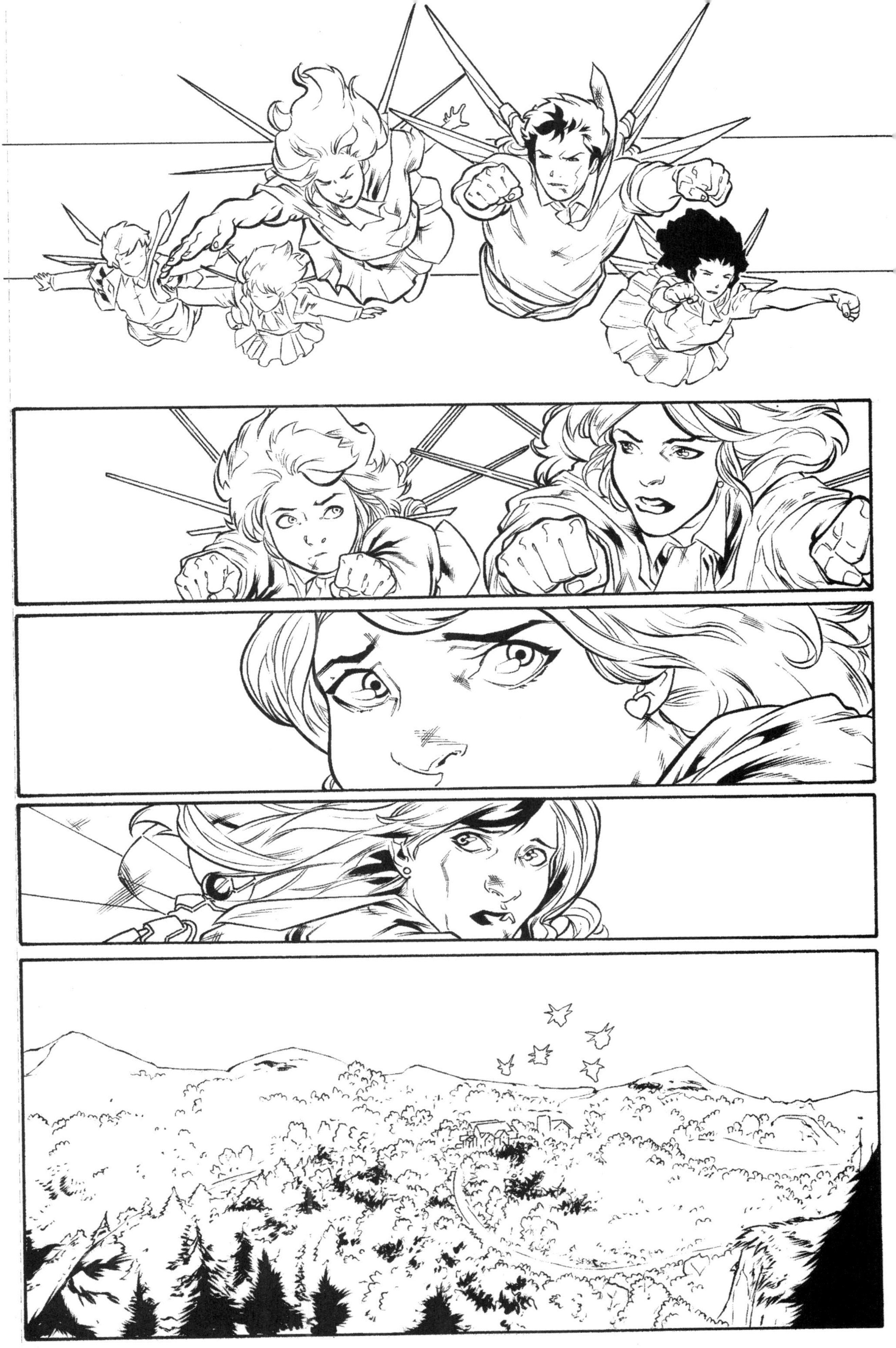

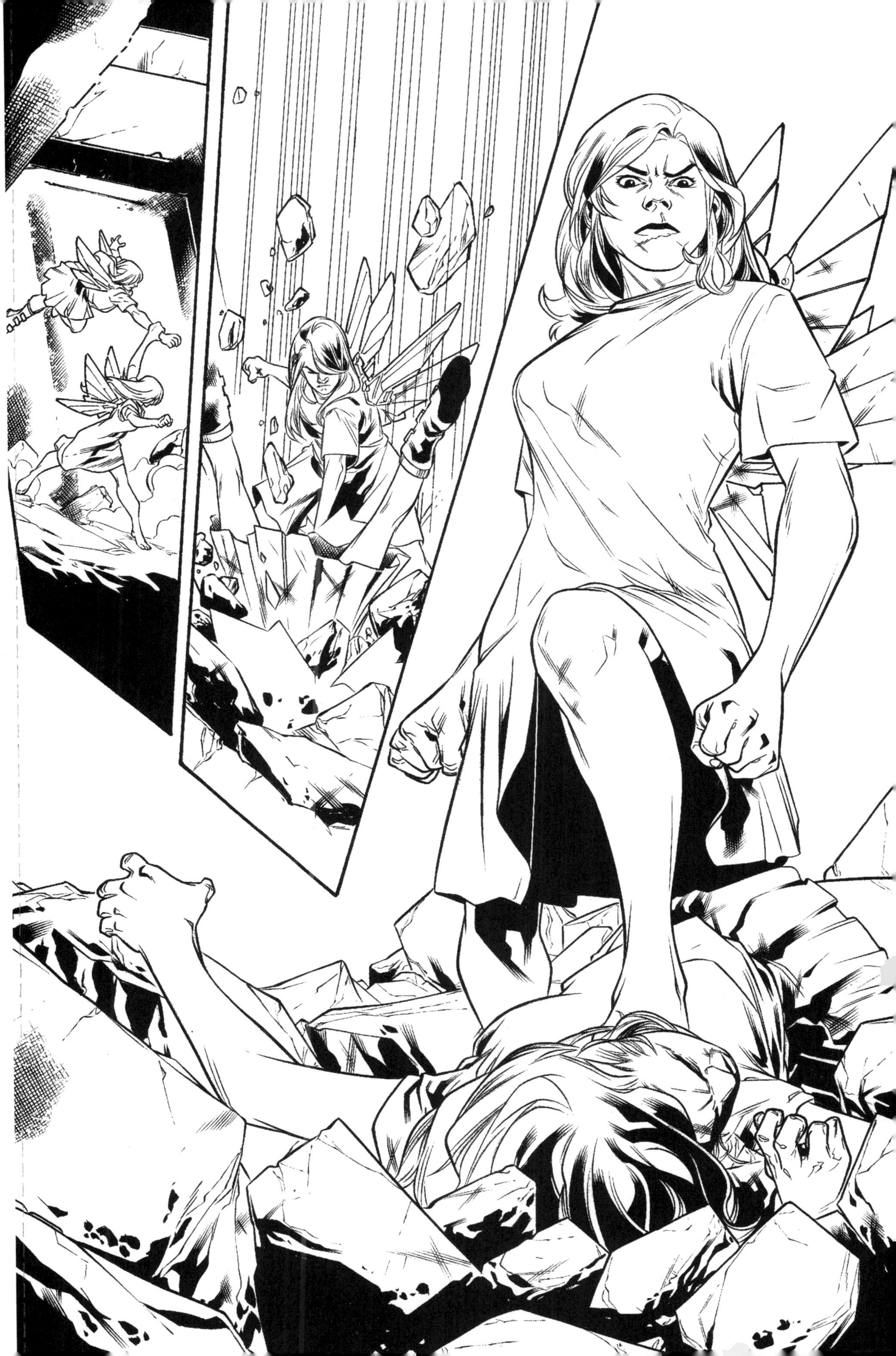

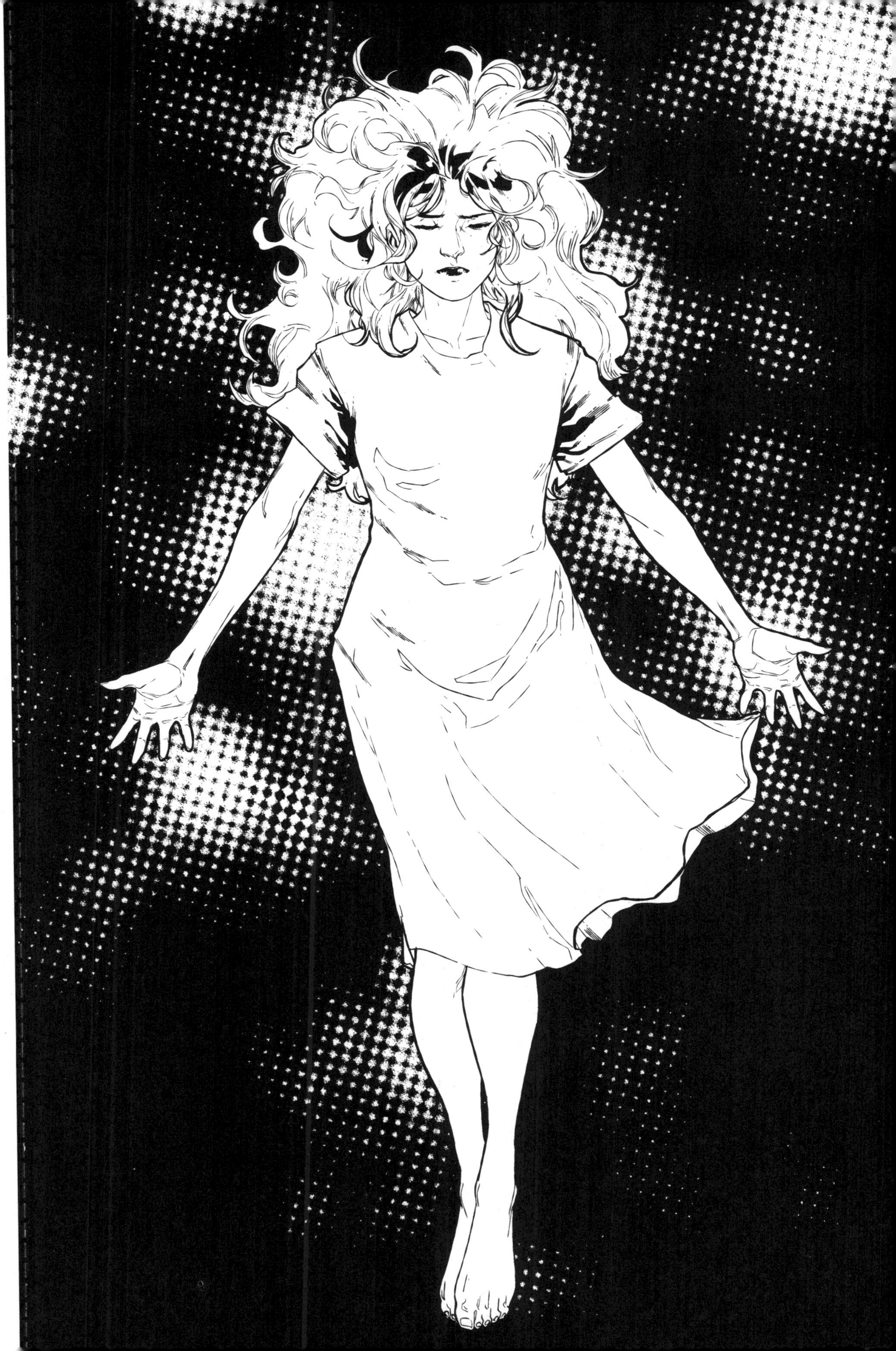

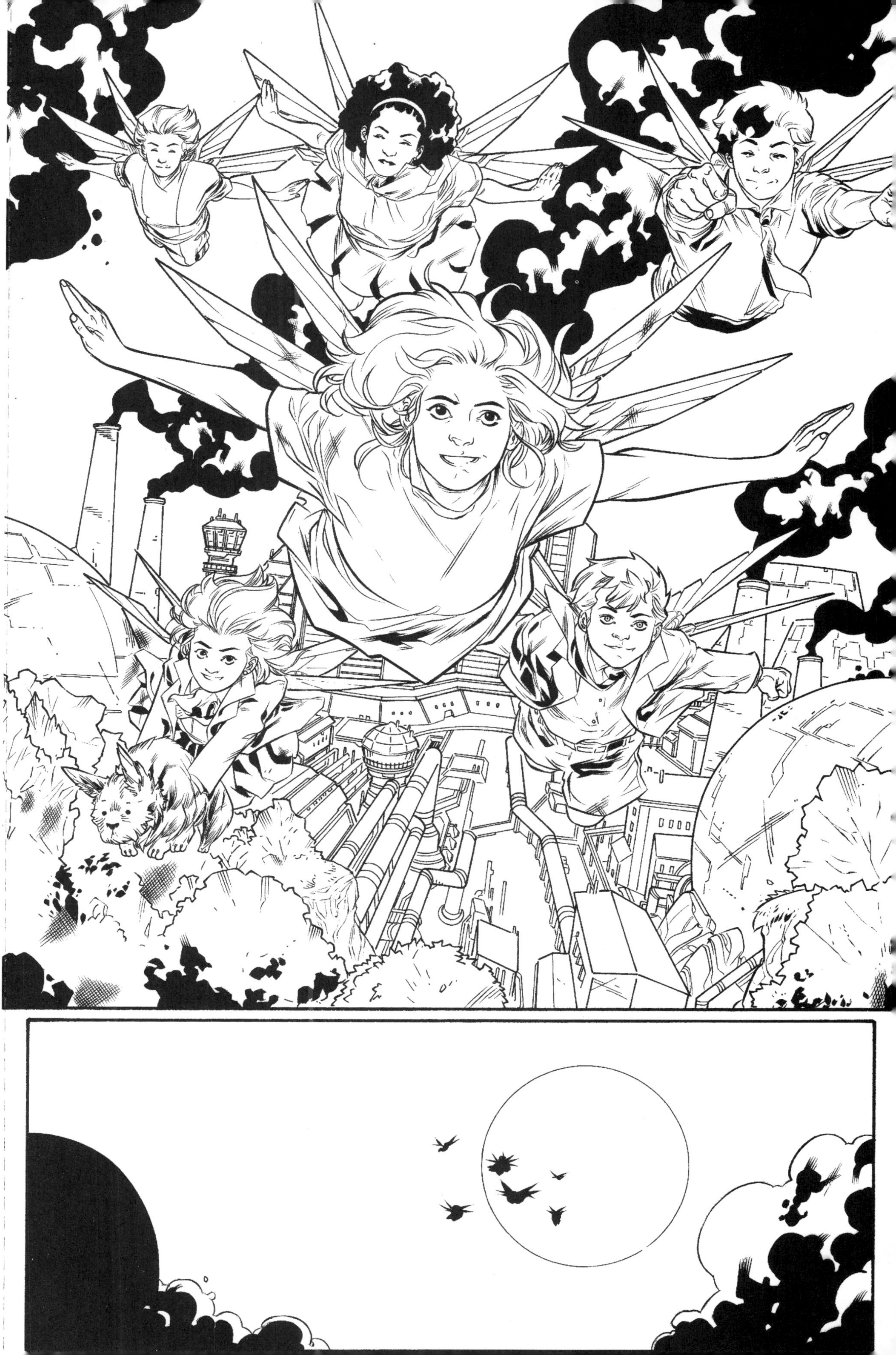

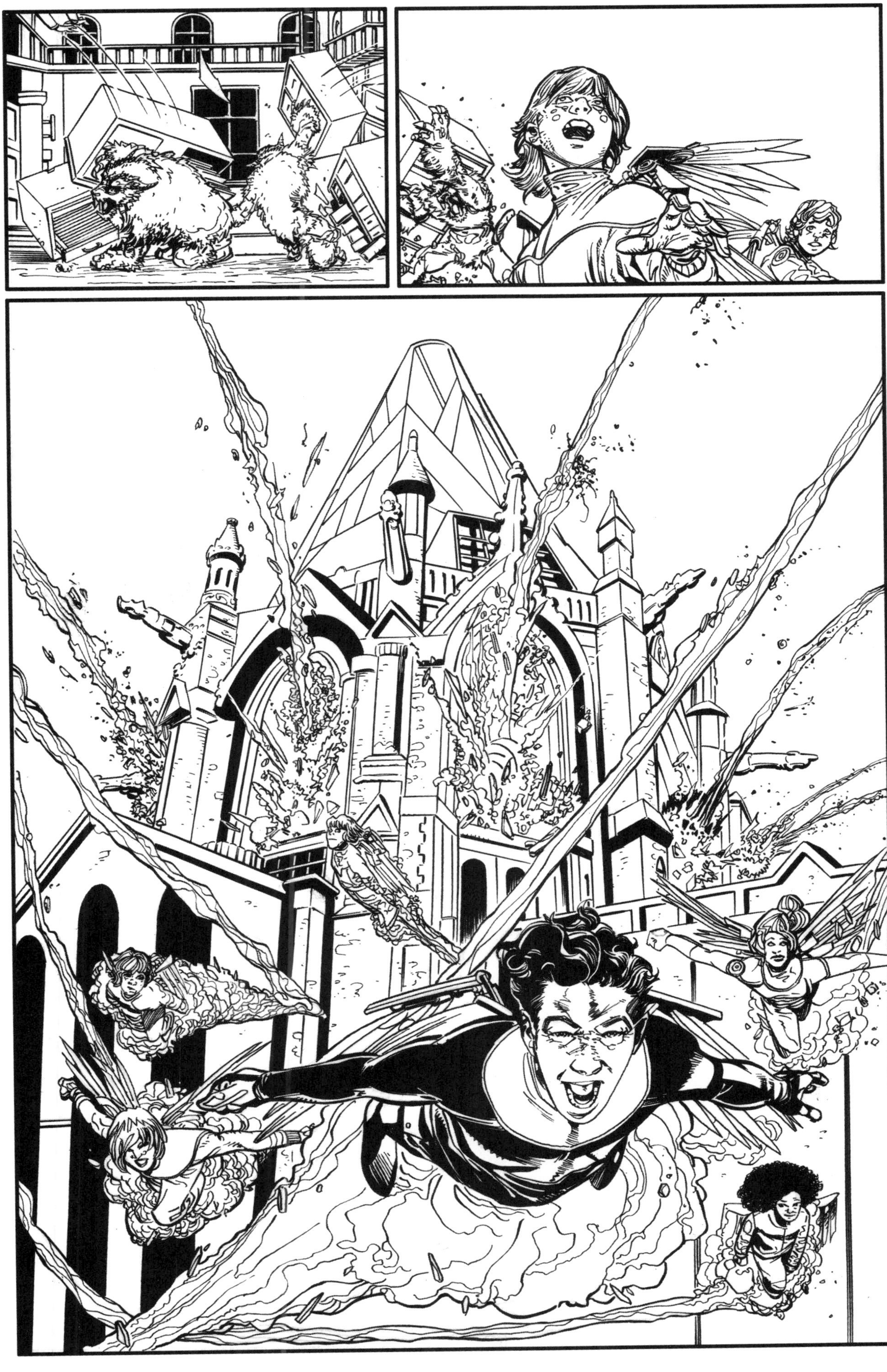

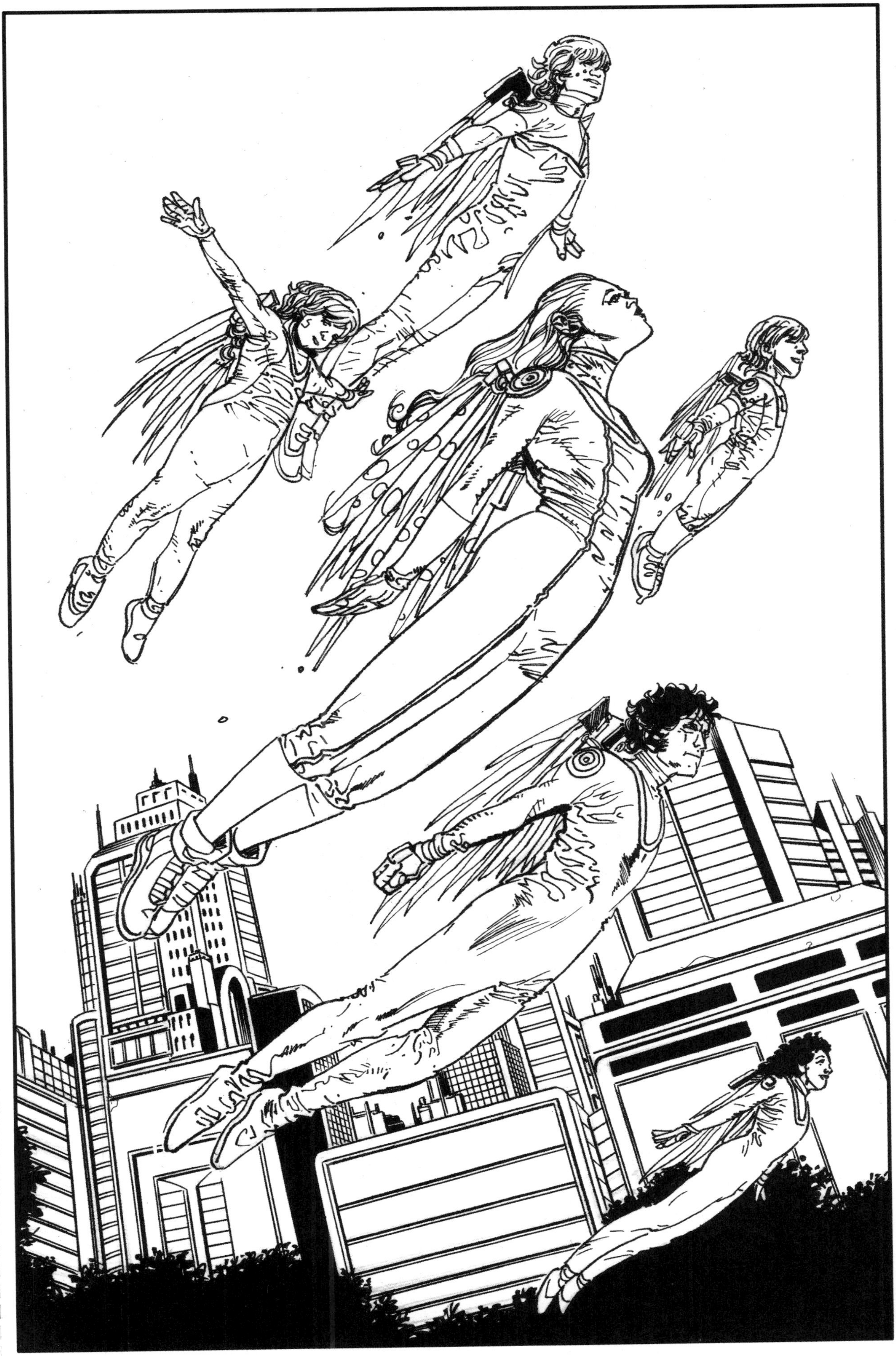

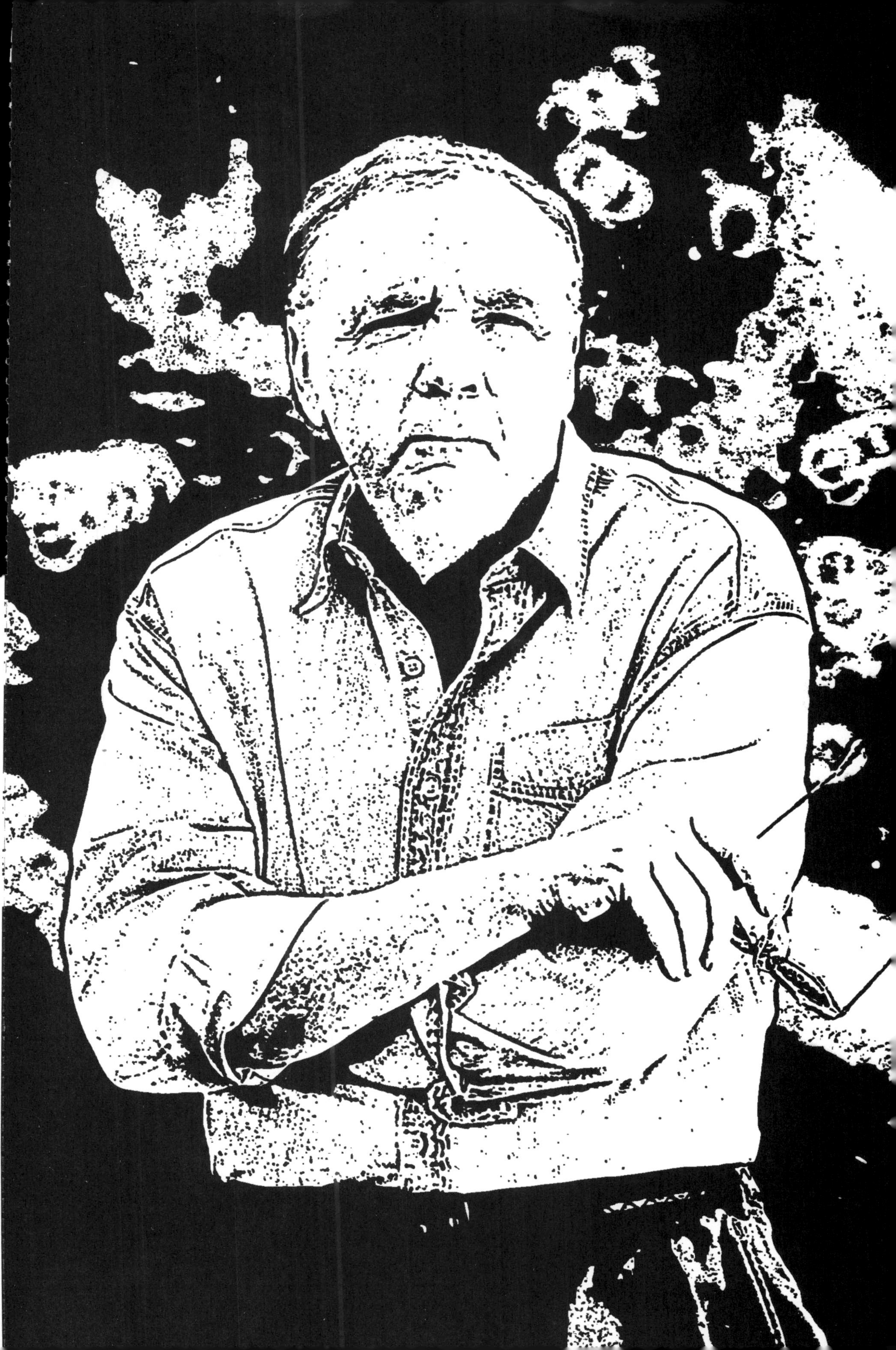